Introduction to the
Problems of Legal Theory

INTRODUCTION TO THE PROBLEMS OF LEGAL THEORY

by

HANS KELSEN

A Translation of the First Edition of the
Reine Rechtslehre or Pure Theory of Law

translated by
Bonnie Litschewski Paulson
and
Stanley L. Paulson

with an Introduction by
Stanley L. Paulson

CLARENDON PRESS · OXFORD

This book has been printed digitally and produced in a standard specification in order to ensure its continuing availability

OXFORD
UNIVERSITY PRESS

Great Clarendon Street, Oxford OX2 6DP

Oxford University Press is a department of the University of Oxford.
It furthers the University's objective of excellence in research, scholarship,
and education by publishing worldwide in

Oxford New York

Auckland Bangkok Buenos Aires Cape Town Chennai
Dar es Salaam Delhi Hong Kong Istanbul Karachi Kolkata
Kuala Lumpur Madrid Melbourne Mexico City Mumbai Nairobi
São Paulo Shanghai Singapore Taipei Tokyo Toronto
with an associated company in Berlin

Oxford is a registered trade mark of Oxford University Press
in the UK and in certain other countries

Published in the United States
by Oxford University Press Inc., New York

ISBN 0-19-826565-4

Translators' Preface

Kelsen published this short treatise in 1934,[1] when the neo-Kantian influence on his work was at its zenith. An earlier, 'constructivist' phase, evident in his *Habilitationsschrift* of 1911,[2] had been displaced over the course of the following decade by his effort, albeit in fits and starts, to provide something approximating a neo-Kantian foundation for his theory. After 1934, Kelsen began to introduce concepts from the empiricist's repertoire, taking over in some of his writings Hume's analysis of causality, for example, and arguing that an *a priori* category of causation would be a step in the wrong direction, away from Hume.[3] Finally, after 1960, Kelsen threw over much of the Pure Theory of Law as we know it from his second and third phases, introducing elements of a volitional or 'will' theory of law to take its place.

If Kelsen's second, neo-Kantian phase represents the Pure Theory of Law in its most characteristic form, then this treatise may well be its central text. And of Kelsen's many statements of the Pure Theory, this one is surely the most accessible.

Translations of the 1934 treatise into Japanese, Bulgarian, Portuguese, and Spanish appeared within a few years of the original, German-language edition. In the first decade after the Second World War, it was also translated into Chinese, Korean, Italian, and French.[4] A translation into Arabic was published in

---

[1] *Reine Rechtslehre. Einleitung in die rechtswissenschaftliche Problematik* (Vienna: Franz Deuticke, 1934, repr. Aalen: Scientia, 1985).

[2] *Hauptprobleme der Staatsrechtslehre* (Tübingen: J.C.B. Mohr, 1911).

[3] See e.g. Kelsen, 'The Emergence of the Causal Law from the Principle of Retribution' (1st pub. 1939), trans. Peter Heath, in Kelsen, *Essays in Legal and Moral Philosophy*, ed. Ota Weinberger (Dordrecht: Reidel, 1973), 165–215, at 196–200.

[4] In *Théorie Pure du Droit*, trans. Henri Thévenaz (Éditions de la Baconnière: Neuchâtel, 1953, repr. with appendices, 1988), Kelsen introduced certain changes.

1986, into Hungarian in 1988. The present text is the first complete translation of the work into English.[5]

The 'second, completely reworked and expanded edition' of Kelsen's *Reine Rechtslehre* or Pure Theory of Law was published in 1960; at nearly 500 pages (including appendices),[6] it is a much longer work than this, the first edition. Indeed, for many purposes the second edition is a new work, appearing as it did at the end of Kelsen's third phase, and reflecting doctrinal changes in his thought. The differences between the two editions, which have generally been treated as separate and distinct works in the secondary literature, have prompted us to take the subtitle of the original text of 1934 as the title for our translation: *Introduction to the Problems of Legal Theory*.[7]

Kelsen had what might be called a 'parenthetical style'. He sometimes qualifies an idea several times in the course of a single sentence, either by simply repeating key phrases or, more often than not, by paring a bit here and plumping up there. German encourages this with its great capacity for extended adjectival constructions and relative clauses, and any attempt at duplication in English would be ill-advised, indeed futile. While we have tried as a rule to stay as close as possible to Kelsen's own formulations, we hope that we have arrived at a respectable compromise, where necessary, between Kelsen's clarity and style in German and the elementary desiderata of clarity and style in English.

Kelsen wrote his book without footnotes. In cases where terminology is problematic, where Kelsen's reference to a text or an individual is not obviously familiar (whoever was the Captain from Köpenick?), or where Kelsen refers to another place in the text, we have added brief footnotes. In a handful of cases, explanations of terms and references are pursued in 'Supplemen-

---

[5] Selections from the work, in a translation by Charles H. Wilson, were published in the *Law Quarterly Review*, 50 (1934), 474–98, and 51 (1935), 517–35.

[6] *Reine Rechtslehre* (Vienna: Franz Deuticke, 1960). In the English-language translation of the 2nd edition, namely, *The Pure Theory of Law*, trans. Max Knight (Berkeley, Calif.: University of California Press, 1967), Kelsen's preface, both lengthy appendices (one on 'The Norms of Justice', the other on 'The Natural Law Theory'), the bibliography, and many of the notes are omitted.

[7] See n. 1 above. On the expressions 'legal theory' and 'legal science', and for more on the title of the translation, see Supplementary Note 1, in appendix I.

tary Notes' at the end of the book. The reader will also find appended a biographical outline (including major publications), and a short annotated bibliography of secondary writings in English.

A word, too, on the Introduction, written by Stanley Paulson. Its first part, an attempt to place Kelsen in the jurisprudential tradition, is elementary. The second part is devoted to an examination of a Kantian or neo-Kantian argument for Kelsen's 'middle way' in jurisprudence. To be sure, there were other influences on Kelsen, among them Georg Jellinek, one of the most prominent figures in German public law, as well as the philosopher Ernst Mach, and the legal theorist Adolf Julius Merkl. Still, most scholars agree that it is the Kantian or neo-Kantian dimension that sets Kelsen's theory apart from run-of-the-mill legal positivism, giving it a special claim on our attention.

Material in the Introduction appeared in a German-language essay by Paulson in *Rechtstheorie*, and is adapted for use here with the permission of the publisher, Duncker & Humblot (Berlin). The text of Xenophon's dialogue between Pericles and Alcibiades (in the Introduction) is drawn from George C. Calhoun, *Introduction to Greek Legal Science*, and is used here with the permission of the publisher, the Oxford University Press. Material in the last of the Supplementary Notes appeared in Paulson's review, in the *American Journal of Comparative Law*, of Mario G. Losano's *Studien zu Jhering und Gerber*; it is used here with the permission of the *Journal*'s editor.

We extend our heartfelt thanks to friends and colleagues—in the United States, the United Kingdom, Austria, Germany, and Poland—who asked and answered questions, read different versions of our often rough draft, and offered us welcome encouragement. Two friends in particular gave us many hours of helpful criticism and discussion, and we thank them here by name—Thomas D. Eisele and Alexander Somek. For valuable references for the biographical outline, and for conversations about Hans Kelsen's life going well beyond what we have distilled for use here, we are indebted to Maria Kelsen Feder. And we thank Marcia Denenholz for her unflagging patience and precision at the computer. Most of the work on the translation was completed during Stanley Paulson's tenure in Münster as Humboldt Fellow, and he remains grateful to the Alexander von Humboldt Foundation (Bonn – Bad Godesberg) for its support.

B.L.P. and S.L.P.
St Louis
December 1990

Contents

Abbreviations

CPR — Immanuel Kant, *Critique of Pure Reason*, trans. Norman Kemp Smith (London: Macmillan, 1929).

HP — Hans Kelsen, *Hauptprobleme der Staatsrechtslehre* (Tübingen: J.C.B. Mohr, 1911). In the second printing (Tübingen: J.C.B. Mohr, 1923, repr. Aalen: Scientia, 1960), Kelsen adds a new foreword; the text itself is unchanged.

Phil. Fds. — Hans Kelsen, *Philosophical Foundations of Natural Law Theory and Legal Positivism* (first published in 1928), trans. Wolfgang H. Kraus, as an appendix to Kelsen, *General Theory of Law and State* (Cambridge, Mass.: Harvard UP, 1945), 389–445.

Proleg. — Immanuel Kant, *Prolegomena to any Future Metaphysics*, trans. Peter G. Lucas (Manchester: Manchester UP, 1953).

WS I, II — *Die Wiener rechtstheoretische Schule. Schriften von Hans Kelsen, Adolf Merkl, Alfred Verdross*, ed. Hans Klecatsky *et al.*, vols. i–ii (Vienna: Europa Verlag, 1968).

ZöR — *Zeitschrift für öffentliches Recht (Journal of Public Law)*, Vienna. Kelsen founded the journal in 1919, and served first as editor-in-chief and then (until his resignation in 1934) as a member of the editorial board.

We have occasionally made changes in the existing English-language translations of quoted material.

Introduction

The American legal theorist Roscoe Pound wrote in 1934 that Hans Kelsen was 'unquestionably the leading jurist of the time'.[1] A quarter of a century later, the English legal philosopher H. L. A. Hart described Kelsen as 'the most stimulating writer on analytical jurisprudence of our day'.[2] And another quarter of a century later, the Finnish philosopher and logician Georg Henrik von Wright compared Kelsen with Max Weber; it is these two thinkers, he wrote, 'who have most deeply influenced . . . social science' in this century.[3] Other writers appraised Kelsen's work in caustic terms. Many in America and England dismissed his Pure Theory of Law as 'utterly sterile', 'barren', amounting to an 'exercise in logic and not in life'.[4] During the Weimar period in Germany, the high point of Kelsen's own role in debates on politics and law in the German-speaking world, writers across the political spectrum contended that the Pure Theory was a failure.[5]

[1] Roscoe Pound, 'Law and the Science of Law in Recent Theories', *Yale Law Journal*, 43 (1933–4), 525–36, at 532.

[2] H. L. A. Hart, 'Kelsen Visited', *UCLA Law Review*, 10 (1962–3), 709–28, at 728, repr. in Hart, *Essays in Jurisprudence and Philosophy* (Oxford: Clarendon Press, 1983), 283–308, at 308. (In the essay Hart develops themes that figured in his debate with Kelsen, held at the University of California, Berkeley, in 1961.)

[3] Georg Henrik von Wright, 'Is and Ought', in *Man, Law and Modern Forms of Life*, ed. Eugenio Bulygin *et al.* (Dordrecht: Reidel, 1985), 263–81, at 263.

[4] See, respectively, Karl N. Llewellyn, *Jurisprudence. Realism in Theory and Practice* (Chicago: University of Chicago Press, 1962), 356; C. K. Allen, *Law in the Making*, 7th edn. (Oxford: Clarendon Press, 1964), 57 (the lines on Kelsen first appeared in the 3rd edition (1939), 51); and Harold J. Laski, *A Grammar of Politics*, 4th edn. (London: Allen & Unwin, 1938), p. vi. Laski, however, had an altogether positive impression of Kelsen personally; writing to Holmes about his visit to the International Institute of Public Law in Paris in the spring of 1932, he remarks: 'Of those I met there, Kelsen of Cologne, certainly the first German jurist of the day, was the most interesting. A profound philosophic mind, quick, agile, and widely read.' *Holmes–Laski Letters*, ed. Mark DeWolfe Howe, vol. ii (Cambridge, Mass.: Harvard UP, 1953), 1376.

[5] On the right, Carl Schmitt wrote that in Kelsen's theory the notions of

A point on which all these writers would agree is that Kelsen was indeed important, a theorist to be reckoned with. To appreciate Kelsen's importance, one must consider his work in the context of the tradition it addresses. According to the received opinion, the Pure Theory of Law stands in sharp contrast to traditional natural law theory. This is of course true; however, as I suggest below, there is more to the relation between these theories than meets the eye.[6] And the question of Kelsen's relation to traditional legal positivism is still more difficult. All too frequently, he is labelled as just another proponent of traditional legal positivism,[7] a label that fails to do justice, in particular, to the normativist dimension of his theory. In fact, it is precisely this normativist dimension that sets the Pure Theory apart from the reductive or 'naturalistic' bent of most of the work done by Kelsen's predecessors in the legal positivist camp.[8] One might well speculate that this difference explains better than anything else the extraordinary interest in Kelsen. While he receives a generally sympathetic reading from those who find the normativist dimension of his Pure Theory promising or at least suggestive, he elicits a negative, even hostile

'ought' and normativity are 'taken over by the tautology of raw factuality'; 'this', Schmitt concluded grimly, 'is positivism.' Carl Schmitt, *Verfassungslehre* (Munich and Leipzig: Duncker & Humblot, 1928), 8–9. On the left, Hermann Heller argued: 'Since, according to Kelsen, the state completely reduces to the law, and the state *qua* legal subject is nothing but "the law *qua* subject", Kelsen's legal norms must create and sustain themselves, which means that they are devoid of positivity (*Positivität*). Kelsen's mystical "self-actuation of the law" leads ultimately "to the *basic norm*, the foundation of the unity of the legal system in its self-actuation". Since the basic norm is known to be a disguise for the non-normative will of the state, Kelsenian law lacks not only positivity but also normativity.' Hermann Heller, *Staatslehre*, ed. Gerhart Niemeyer (Leiden: Sijthoff, 1934), 198, repr. in Heller, *Gesammelte Schriften*, ed. Martin Drath *et al.*, vol. iii (Leiden: Sijthoff, 1971), 79–395, at 305. Heller's quotation in the second sentence is from Kelsen, *Allgemeine Staatslehre* (Berlin: Springer, 1925, repr. Bad Homburg v. d. Höhe: Max Gehlen, 1966), at 249.

   [6] See the text corresponding to n. 20 below.
   [7] R. K. Gooch voices a widely held opinion when he writes that 'it seems fair to say that Herr Kelsen is essentially a Neo-Austinian'. Gooch, Book Review: Hans Kelsen, *General Theory of Law and State*, in *Virginia Law Review*, 32 (1945–6), 212–15, at 214.
   [8] Kelsen, speaking for himself, Rudolf Stammler, and others, writes that in taking cues from 'Kant's transcendental philosophy', we are combating a 'naïve empiristic naturalism'. Kelsen, 'Rechtswissenschaft und Recht', *ZöR*, 3 (1922), 103–235, at 104, repr. in Fritz Sander and Hans Kelsen, *Die Rolle des Neukantianismus in der Reinen Rechtslehre*, ed. Stanley L. Paulson (Aalen: Scientia, 1988), 279–411, at 280.

reaction from those who see him as somehow worse than the old-guard legal positivists, having pretended to be something else.[9]

The key to the normativist dimension of the Pure Theory, particularly in Kelsen's writings of the 1920s and early 1930s, is a Kantian argument. To set the stage for the argument, I trace, in Part I of this introduction, Kelsen's steps as he constructs and then resolves what I shall call the jurisprudential antinomy. The antinomy represents, to be sure, not a reconstruction of an argument expressly developed by Kelsen but, rather, my interpretation of his strategy. I offer the antinomy as a means of highlighting those theses in Kelsen's Pure Theory that distinguish it from both traditional natural law theory and traditional legal positivism, and as a means of pinpointing what Kelsen would have to show to make a case on behalf of his ostensibly distinct theory, a middle way between the traditional theories.

In Part II of the Introduction, I consider the case Kelsen makes, his Kantian argument. More precisely, Kelsen's argument is a neo-Kantian or 'regressive' version of Kant's transcendental argument. And I show that the problems familiar from the neo-Kantians' own formulations of the transcendental argument turn up again in Kelsen's formulation.

PART I. THE JURISPRUDENTIAL ANTINOMY

Kelsen would have his Pure Theory of Law understood as a theory of legal cognition, of legal knowledge. He writes again and again that the sole aim of the Pure Theory is cognition or knowledge of its object, precisely specified as the law itself. In constructing a theory of specifically legal cognition, Kelsen's special task is to ward off the 'foreign elements' that, he believes, have led legal theory astray so often in the past. Jurists and legal scholars have become entangled in 'alien' disciplines—in ethics and theology, in psychology and biology.[10] And by venturing into these non-legal fields in search of answers to legal questions, they have been chasing a will-o'-the-wisp.

---

[9] This latter attitude is reflected in the writings of some of Kelsen's Weimar critics (see n. 5 above).

[10] See § 1 of the present text.

Why is it that Kelsen, in the name of legal theory, resists the inclination to turn to ethics, psychology, and the like for help on legal questions? A closer look at his allusions to what he terms 'alien' fields is telling. The discipline known as the 'specific science of law' must be 'distinguished from the philosophy of justice on the one hand and from sociology, or the cognition of social reality, on the other'.[11] Kelsen's allusions, here, amount to thinly disguised references to the main competing views in the Western tradition in jurisprudence and legal philosophy, and it is from these traditional views that a 'pure' theory of law must be sharply distinguished. Kelsen expresses the same notion at greater length in an early work:

the purity of the theory . . . is to be secured in two directions. It is to be secured against the claims of a so-called 'sociological' point of view, which uses the methods of the causal sciences to appropriate the law as a part of nature. And the purity of the theory is to be secured against the claims of the natural law theory, which . . . takes legal theory out of the realm of positive legal norms and into the realm of ethico-political postulates.[12]

Three points, drawn in large part from the texts quoted above, hint at a strategy Kelsen employs generally. The first point is historical. Kelsen, along with many others, understands the Western tradition in jurisprudence and legal philosophy in terms of two basic types of theory—natural law theory, and an empirical, sociological, or 'positivist' theory of law. In natural law theory, the law is seen as necessarily subject to moral constraints; in the empirico-positivist theory, it is seen as part of the world of fact or nature.

A second point, building on the first and going beyond the view expressed in the texts quoted above, has philosophical import. Many in the tradition have understood natural law theory and the empirico-positivist theory as not only mutually exclusive, but also jointly exhaustive of the possibilities. Thus understood, the two types of theory together rule out any third

---

[11] Kelsen, 'The Pure Theory of Law and Analytical Jurisprudence', *Harvard Law Review*, 55 (1941–2), 44–70, at 44, repr. in Kelsen, *What is Justice?* (Berkeley, Calif.: University of California Press, 1957), 266–87, 390 (notes), at 266.

[12] *HP*, 2nd printing (Tübingen: J. C. B. Mohr, 1923), 'Foreword to the Second Printing', p. v.

possibility *(tertium non datur)*. Pretenders—theories that purport to be distinct from both traditional theories—turn out to be disguised versions of the one or the other.

The third point, stemming, as the first does, directly from the texts quoted above, is Kelsen's rejection of both traditional theories. Neither natural law theory nor the empirico-positivist theory is defensible. Proponents confuse the law with morality and with fact respectively, failing to see that the law has a 'specific meaning'[13] of its own.

If one takes the second and third points together, things become interesting. For if one holds that the two traditional types of theory together exhaust the field, precluding any third type of theory, and if one holds, furthermore, that neither type of theory is defensible, then one faces an antinomy—the *jurisprudential antinomy*, as I shall call it.

Clearly, something has to give. The antinomy blocks every move, and must be resolved before one can go forward. Kelsen (as we shall see below) resolves the antinomy by showing that the traditional theories are not exhaustive of the field after all. He is then in a position to introduce his alternative to the traditional theories—the Pure Theory of Law. His theory is 'pure'[14] in being free of the 'foreign elements' of both types of traditional theory; it hinges neither on considerations of morality nor on matters of fact.

---

[13] See § 16 of the present text. Perhaps the most useful commentary on this elusive notion is Alf Ross, *Towards a Realistic Jurisprudence*, trans. Annie I. Fausbøll (Copenhagen: Einar Munksgaard, 1946, repr. Aalen: Scientia, 1989), at 39–48.

[14] As Kant writes: 'Any knowledge is entitled pure, if it be not mixed with anything extraneous.' *CPR* A11–12 (sentence omitted in B). The Kantian notion is evident in what was perhaps the most immediate influence on Kelsen vis-à-vis 'purity', namely, the positivist tradition in German public law. There, 'purity' meant freedom from *methodological syncretism* (Gk. '*synkretismos*', 'combination'), and the phrase 'methodological syncretism' was used to refer to an illegitimate combining or fusion of different methods. As Georg Jellinek put it: 'If one has comprehended the general difference between the jurist's conceptual sphere and the objective sphere of natural processes and events, one will appreciate the inadmissibility of transferring the cognitive method of the latter over to the former. Among the vices of the scientific enterprise of our day is the vice of methodological syncretism.' Jellinek, *System der subjektiven öffentlichen Rechte*, 2nd edn. (Tübingen: J. C. B. Mohr, 1905, repr. Aalen: Scientia, 1979), 17.

Although freedom from methodological syncretism was a point on which all of Kelsen's positivist precursors in German public law—Carl Friedrich von Gerber, xxii Introduction

Generating the Antinomy: Morality Thesis and Separability
Thesis

Before turning to some details of Kelsen's resolution of the
jurisprudential antinomy, it will be useful to take a closer look at
the antinomy itself. As reported by Xenophon, the following
dialogue between Pericles and Alcibiades[15] illustrates the competing positions that generate the antinomy.

It is said that Alcibiades, before he was twenty, had a conversation
with Pericles, his guardian and the head of the Athenian state, on the
subject of the law.
'Tell me, Pericles,' Alcibiades asked, 'can you explain to me what a
law is?'
'Of course I can,' answered Pericles.
'Then please do so,' said Alcibiades. 'For when I hear people praised
for being law-abiding, I am of the opinion that no man can rightly be
praised in this way if he does not know what a law is.'
'What you want is nothing difficult, Alcibiades—to know what a law
is. All these are laws, all that the people in assembly approve and enact,
setting out what is or is not to be done.'
'With the idea that good is to be done, or bad?'
'Of course good is to be done, my boy, not bad!' Pericles declared.
'But if it is not the people, if, as in an oligarchy, it is a minority who
assemble and enact what is or is not to be done, what are these?'
'Everything the ruling power in the state enacts with due deliberation,
enjoining what is to be done, is called a law,' intoned Pericles.
'Then if a despot, being the ruling power in the state, enacts what the

Paul Laband, and Jellinek—placed great weight, Laband's statement on a 'pure'
legal method was the one that became notorious. Laband claims that one task of
legal science is 'the construction of legal institutes', which means 'tracing
particular legal norms (*Rechtssätze*) back to more general concepts and, on the
other hand, deriving the consequences of these concepts'. He goes on to say that
'to attain this end there is no means but logic, no means can replace logic; all
historical, political, and philosophical considerations—however valuable they
may be in and of themselves—are without significance [for this enquiry], and
serve all too often to obscure the lack of "constructivistic" work'. Paul Laband,
Das Staatsrecht des Deutschen Reiches, vol. i, 2nd edn. (Freiburg: J. C. B. Mohr,
1888), p. xi. (See Supplementary Note 7 in appendix I for a few lines on the
constructivistic origins of work such as Laband's.)
[15] Xenophon's dialogue does not purport to be biographical; in particular, the
Alcibiades of the dialogue is not to be confused with the historical Alcibiades. See
e.g. Erik Wolf, *Rechtsphilosophie der Sokratik und Rechtsdichtung der alten
Komödie*, vol. iii, pt. 1, of *Griechisches Rechtsdenken* (Frankfurt: Vittorio
Klostermann, 1954), at 129.

citizens are to do, is this, too, a law?'

'Yes, everything a despot, as ruler, enacts,' answered Pericles, 'this, too, is called a law.'

'But what is force, the negation of law, Pericles? Is it not when the stronger compels the weaker to do his will, not by persuasion but by force?'

'Yes, that is my opinion,' agreed Pericles.

'Then everything a despot enacts and compels the citizens to do, without persuasion, is the negation of law?'

'Correct,' said Pericles. 'I retract my statement that everything a despot enacts is a law, for without persuasion, his enactments are not law.'

'And what the minority enact, not by persuading the majority but through superior power, are we or are we not to call it force?'

'I believe', answered Pericles, 'that without persuasion, whatever one compels another to do—whether by enactment or otherwise—is force rather than law.'

'Then whatever the people as a whole enact, not by persuasion but by being stronger than the owners of property, this, too, would be force rather than law?'

'Let me tell you, Alcibiades, when I was your age I, too, was good at this sort of thing. We used to practise just the sort of clever quibbling I think you are practising right now.'

'How I should like to have known you in those days, Pericles, when you were in your prime!'[16]

Pericles begins the dialogue confidently, stating that law is what the people 'in assembly approve and enact'. Responding to pointed questions from Alcibiades, however, he is driven to stating that 'enactment' or issuance is enough in itself, even where it is not the people in assembly who are making the laws, but rather some minority or even a despot. Pericles appears to be saying that law is simply an institutionalized expression of the existing power relations, and Alcibiades suggests in his rejoinder that Pericles has gone too far. Pericles sees that indeed he has, and beats a hasty retreat.

---

[16] Xenophon, *Memorabilia*, I. ii. 40–6, trans. George C. Calhoun, in Calhoun, *Introduction to Greek Legal Science* (Oxford: Clarendon Press, 1944, repr. Scientia: Aalen, 1977), 78–80 (with changes). The most recent translation is Xenophon, *Conversations of Socrates*, trans. Hugh Tredennick and Robin Waterfield (London: Penguin, 1990), at 80–1. I am grateful to my friend Timothy O'Hagan for his advice on the rendering of the dialogue.

On what basis does Alcibiades challenge the statement that the despot's enactment is law? The answer must ultimately be given in terms of morality. Law is legitimate only if the ruler has a right to enact or issue it, and he has that right only if the citizens are persuaded to consent thereto, that is, only if he rules by persuasion and not by force. In modern parlance: for the ruler to proceed without the consent of the citizens is tantamount to a denial of their autonomy, and the significance of autonomy can only be explicated in moral terms.

The dialogue serves to illustrate the positions—thesis and antithesis—that generate the jurisprudential antinomy. Alcibiades' position represents the thesis, which I shall call the *morality thesis*. It gives expression to the idea that the nature of law is explicated ultimately in moral terms. For the sake of contrast with the antithesis, the morality thesis might be said to claim the inseparability of law and morality.

The antithesis, claiming the separability of law and morality, is called the *separability thesis*.[17] It might be argued that Pericles' initial efforts to defend the view that law is simply an expression of power reflect different versions of the separability thesis. Although everyone grants that there are indeed ties between law and morality, the separability thesis rejects the view that these ties are conceptual or *a priori* in character. The legal validity of, say, a statutory provision does not depend on the conformity of the provision to some overriding moral precept; it depends, rather, on the satisfaction of the conditions associated with the lawmaking process. Thus, the claim that the nature of law is to be explicated in moral terms is without basis—or so the proponent of the separability thesis contends.

The jurisprudential antinomy does not arise, however, simply from a juxtaposition of the morality and separability theses. Rather, it arises from a twofold assumption: first, that the morality thesis stands for natural law theory, and the separability thesis for the empirico-positivist theory, and, second, that the

---

[17] 'Separability thesis' is standard nomenclature, reflecting above all H. L. A. Hart's work; see Hart, 'Positivism and the Separation of Law and Morals', *Harvard Law Review*, 71 (1957–8), 593–629, repr. in Hart, *Essays* (n. 2 above), 49–87. On problems associated with the separability thesis, see e.g. David Lyons, 'Moral Aspects of Legal Theory', *Midwest Studies in Philosophy*, 7 (1982), 223–54; and Robert Alexy, 'On Necessary Relations between Law and Morality', *Ratio Juris*, 2 (1989), 168–84.

juxtaposition of the theses therefore gives expression to a corresponding juxtaposition of the traditional theories themselves. If the assumption is correct, then the traditional theories are not only mutually exclusive but also jointly exhaustive of the possibilities. Finally, lest we forget the all-important antinomic turn in the argument, neither natural law theory nor the empirico-positivist theory is defensible. Kelsen rejects them both, and in doing so he faces squarely the jurisprudential antinomy.

Resolving the Antinomy: Reductive Thesis and Normativity Thesis

Kelsen's resolution of the jurisprudential antinomy stems from the observation, fundamental here, that while the traditional theories have been stated in terms of the morality and separability theses alone, there are in fact four theses to reckon with, and not just two. The traditional reading, spelled out solely in terms of the relation between law and morality, fails to take account of a second issue, the relation between law and fact. Once this second issue is recognized, its theses—combined in various ways with the original theses—give the lie to the notion that natural law theory and the empirico-positivist theory could together exhaust the field, that their juxtaposition could give rise to an antinomy.

To see what the issue of the relation between law and fact comes to, it is useful to examine the two theses associated with it. The *reductive thesis* claims that law is explicated ultimately in factual terms; it claims, in a word, the inseparability of law and fact.[18] Its antithesis, the *normativity thesis*, claims the separability of law and fact.[19] The reductive thesis, by definition, is an aspect of the empirico-positivist theory, and the normativity

---

[18] Kelsen interprets a great many of his predecessors and contemporaries in reductive terms, some for the good reason that they were reductive theorists plain and simple (e.g. Felix Somló, the 'Continental Austin', and see Kelsen, *Das Problem der Souveränität* (Tübingen: J. C. B. Mohr, 1920), 31–6), others for the less obvious reason that what survived of their theories in the wake of Kelsen's critique was reductive in nature (e.g. Rudolf Stammler, and see *HP*, 57–63).

[19] On Kelsen's conception of normativity generally, see §§ 8, 16 of the present text.

thesis, more by implication than by express argument, reflects a part of natural law theory.[20]

The scheme below illustrates, for Kelsen's purposes, the possibilities that emerge once the theses on the relation between law and fact are joined to the traditional theses on the relation between law and morality.

law law and morality	law and fact	*normativity thesis* (separability of law and fact)	*reductive thesis* (inseparability of law and fact)
morality thesis (inseparability of law and morality)		natural law theory	
separability thesis (separability of law and morality)		Kelsen's Pure Theory of Law	empirico-positivist theory of law

The theses listed vertically specify relations between law and morality; those listed horizontally specify relations between law and fact. Taking up the traditional theories, the idea is to characterize each in terms of two theses. Natural law theory brings together the morality thesis and the normativity thesis. The empirico-positivist theory brings together the separability thesis and the reductive thesis. What of the other positions? Kelsen's Pure Theory of Law is an attempt to bring together the separability thesis and the normativity thesis. And the single left-over position, not surprisingly, has no takers. For if the morality thesis is interpreted, as in the tradition, in terms of a critical, '*non*-naturalistic' morality, then its juxtaposition with the reductive or 'naturalistic' thesis would amount to a contradiction in terms.

The scheme illustrates Kelsen's resolution of the jurisprudential antinomy. Once the additional theses are introduced, it becomes clear that the opposition of the traditional theories is not that of genuine contradictories—the morality and separability theses. Rather, the four theses lend themselves to various

[20] See *HP*, at 7, where Kelsen tacitly acknowledges a tie between the normativity thesis and traditional natural law theory; see also Joseph Raz, who writes in *The Authority of Law* (Oxford: Clarendon Press, 1979), at 144, that Kelsen, though rejecting natural law theories, 'consistently uses the natural law concept of normativity, i.e. the concept of justified normativity'.

combinations, and the opposition of pairs of theses is simply that of contraries. The introduction of the additional theses thus gives the lie to the antinomic choice—the idea, that is, that the only choice is between the original two theses, both indefensible.

Mistaken Interpretations of the Scheme

It would be misleading, to be sure, to take the scheme too literally, as though Kelsen's theory were equidistant from traditional natural law theory and the traditional empirico-positivist theory. In fact, Kelsen sees himself as a champion of legal positivism, defends the separability thesis with a vengeance, and readily acknowledges his debt to the juridico-positivist tradition.[21] His legal positivism, however, is positivism with a difference: instead of the old reductive thesis, Kelsen defends a normativity thesis—and does so without appealing to the morality thesis of natural law. In a word, Kelsen's 'positivism with a difference' rests on his defence of a combination of theses different from that defended by the positivists of the tradition.

The scheme may be misleading in another way. It may appear to be addressing the paucity of the tradition by offering a full set of options for possible legal theories. Indeed, if one were to introduce the four theses as akin to variables ('A', 'B', 'C', and 'D'), and were then to pursue not only all of the possible interpretations of each thesis, but also all of the possible combinations of these different interpretations, one could perhaps make a *prima facie* claim to completeness.[22] But nothing of the sort is intended here.

Rather, in introducing the four theses of the scheme I am taking my cues from Kelsen's view of their respective historical

---

[21] See Kelsen's Preface to the present text, and also § 12. Similarly, writing in 1925: 'I see, more clearly than before, how very much my own work rests on that of my predecessors . . . Karl Friedrich von Gerber, Paul Laband, and Georg Jellinek,' in the positivist tradition of 19th-century German public law. Kelsen, *Allgemeine Staatslehre* (n. 5 above), Preface, at p. vii.

[22] Alexy, in 'On Necessary Relations between Law and Morality' (n. 17 above), at 171–4, presses hard on the ambiguities inherent in the separability thesis (ambiguities between substance and procedure, between observer and participant, etc.) and arrives at 64 possible readings. Even if many of these have no application, as Alexy readily grants, the exercise is telling on the question of what a *prima facie* claim to completeness might come to.

interpretations. An example already alluded to is the morality thesis: traditional natural law theory interprets the morality thesis in terms of a 'non-naturalistic', critical moral theory. This historical interpretation is right for my purposes here, but it hardly exhausts the possibilities for interpreting the thesis.

Given the more or less familiar interpretation of each thesis, certain logical ties between the theses suggest themselves. Expressed as questions, the following possible connections are of special interest, affording, as they do, another view of how Kelsen distinguishes his own position from those of the tradition.

(i) Is the *normativity thesis* derivable from the *morality thesis*?
The tradition: yes
Kelsen: yes

(ii) Turning the question around, is the *morality thesis* derivable from the *normativity thesis*?
The tradition: yes
Kelsen: no

(iii) Is the *separability thesis* derivable from the *reductive thesis*?
The tradition: yes
Kelsen: yes

(iv) Turning the question around, is the *reductive thesis* derivable from the *separability thesis*?
The tradition: yes
Kelsen: no

Kelsen challenges the defenders of traditional natural law theory and the old empirico-positivist theory. Specifically, he challenges the tradition in its answers to questions (ii) and (iv). He must deny that the morality thesis can be derived from the normativity thesis, and that the reductive thesis can be derived from the separability thesis, lest the theses on the relation between law and fact collapse into the traditional theses on the relation between law and morality. Such a collapse would be fatal, restoring the juxtaposition of the traditional theories *qua* morality and separability theses, and thus undermining Kelsen's claim to be offering a new theory, conceptually distinct from those of the tradition.

In other words, Kelsen's answers to questions (ii) and (iv) suggest the hypotheses with which he begins—the normativity thesis *without* the morality thesis, and the separability thesis *without* the reductive thesis. But can he make his case? Having precluded an appeal either to the morality thesis or to the reductive thesis, he faces an especially difficult task in defending his alternative.

PART II. KELSEN'S NEO-KANTIAN OR 'REGRESSIVE' ARGUMENT

The alternative that Kelsen offers is a Kantian or neo-Kantian 'middle way'. It is not a reflection of Kant's moral or legal philosophy, which Kelsen believes to have all the trappings of classical natural law theory,[23] but rather a reflection of bits and pieces of Kant's theory of knowledge.[24] And on one reading of Kelsen, the parallel between his theory and Kant's is striking. Kant resolves the first of the mathematical antinomies, posed by the juxtaposition of dogmatic rationalism and sceptical empiricism, by arguing that the notion of 'a world of the senses existing of itself'[25]—existing absolutely—amounts to a self-contradiction, and must be replaced by the notion that the world

[23] 'A complete emancipation from metaphysics was no doubt impossible for a personality as deeply rooted in Christianity as Kant's. This is most evident in his practical philosophy; for it is precisely here, where the emphasis of Christian doctrine lies, that the metaphysical dualism of that doctrine invades Kant's entire system, the same dualism he had fought so vehemently in his theoretical philosophy. At this point, Kant has abandoned his transcendental method, a contradiction in critical idealism that has been noted often enough. And so it is that Kant, *whose transcendental philosophy was destined to provide, in particular, the foundation for a positivist legal and political philosophy,* remained, as a legal philosopher, in the rut of natural law theory. Indeed, his *Foundations of the Metaphysics of Morals* can be regarded as the most nearly perfect expression of classical natural law theory as it developed out of Protestant Christianity during the seventeenth and eighteenth centuries.' *Phil. Fds.* 444–5 (Kelsen's italics).

[24] See e.g. William Ebenstein, *The Pure Theory of Law*, trans. Charles H. Wilson (Madison, Wis.: University of Wisconsin Press, 1945, repr. New York: Rothman, 1969), who offers what is, in the secondary literature, perhaps the most thoroughgoing Kantian interpretation extant of Kelsen's Pure Theory. Within the Vienna School, the most ambitious, albeit short-lived, Kantian theory of legal knowledge stems not from Kelsen but from the *enfant terrible* of the Vienna School, Fritz Sander. Particularly noteworthy is Sander's paper 'Die transzendentale Methode der Rechtsphilosophie und der Begriff der Rechtserfahrung', *ZöR*, 1 (1919–20), 468–507, repr. in Sander and Kelsen, *Die Rolle des Neukantianismus* (n. 8 above), 75–114.

[25] *Proleg.* § 52(c), at p. 107.

exists not 'of itself' but only in relation to mind.[26] Kant works up the latter position, his middle way, in the Transcendental Analytic of the *Critique of Pure Reason*. So too, by showing the possibility of a middle way in legal philosophy, Kelsen resolves the jurisprudential antinomy, generated by the traditional reading of the juxtaposition of natural law theory and the empirico-positivist theory. His next step is to develop just such a middle way, and he does so by means of a Kantian argument.

If Kelsen's Kantian argument is cogent, then his middle way, bringing together the normativity thesis and the separability thesis, represents a genuine alternative to the traditional theories. Thus, the Kantian argument on behalf of a middle way may well hold the key to Kelsen's entire enterprise.

The Transcendental Question

A useful starting point in examining the Kantian argument is the so-called transcendental question. In medieval philosophy, the transcendentals (*unum, bonum, verum*) were familiar as general features of being that transcend classification into genera and species. Departing radically from this tradition, Kant nevertheless retains some of its nomenclature, using 'transcendental'[27] to speak of cognition or knowledge that is concerned 'not so much with the objects of cognition as with how we cognize objects, in so far as this may be possible *a priori*'.[28] And it is this distinctively Kantian reading of 'transcendental'—dismissed by Hegel as 'barbaric terminology', and giving rise, in Vaihinger's words, to 'horrible misinterpretations'[29]—that flags the conditions of the possibility of cognition. Kant's transcendental question asks how such knowledge or cognition is possible.

[26] On the first mathematical antinomy generally, see *CPR*, at A426–38/B454–66, A490–567/B518–95.

[27] The historical developments preparing the way for Kant's reception of the concept of 'transcendental' are traced in Norbert Hinske, 'Die historischen Vorlagen der Kantischen Transzendentalphilosophie', *Archiv für Begriffsgeschichte*, 12 (1968), 86–113, esp. 89–95.

[28] *CPR* B25.

[29] G. W. F. Hegel, *Lectures on the History of Philosophy*, trans. E. S. Haldane and Frances H. Simson, vol. iii (London: Kegan Paul, Trench, Trübner, 1896), 431; Hans Vaihinger, *Commentar zu Kants Kritik der reinen Vernunft*, vol. i (Stuttgart: W. Spemann, 1881, repr. New York: Garland, 1976), 467.

Kelsen, consciously following Kant at this juncture, poses his own transcendental question: 'How is positive law *qua* object of cognition, *qua* object of cognitive legal science, possible?'[30] Kelsen is asking for an argument in support of the *constitutive function* of cognitive legal science. He contends that legal science, in focusing on certain data (acts of will) and cognizing them by means of an 'objective' interpretation, thereby constitutes anew the data drawn from raw statutory material.[31] These cognized, 'objectively' interpreted data take the form of hypothetically formulated or *reconstructed legal norms*,[32] the proper objects of cognition in legal science.

In putting his transcendental question, Kelsen is not asking whether we cognize legal material, whether we know certain legal propositions to be true. Rather, he assumes that we have such knowledge, and is asking how we can have it. To capture something of the peculiarly transcendental twist to Kelsen's question, we might ask: given that we know something to be true, what presupposition is at work? More specifically, what presupposition is at work without which the proposition that we know to be true could not be true?

The Basic Norm and the Transcendental Argument

Kelsen's attempt to answer the transcendental question hinges on an appeal to the basic norm.[33] The intuitive idea behind the basic norm is clear. In all his work, Kelsen championed a hard and fast distinction between 'is' and 'ought', a distinction

---

[30] *Phil. Fds.* 437.

[31] On this aspect of Kelsen's Kantian alternative, namely, the notion of the constitutive function of cognitive legal science, there is something of a consensus among Kelsen's contemporaries, see e.g. Franz Weyr, 'Reine Rechtslehre und Verwaltungsrecht', in *Gesellschaft, Staat und Recht. Untersuchungen zur Reinen Rechtslehre*, ed. Alfred Verdross (Vienna: Springer, 1931, repr. Frankfurt: Sauer & Auvermann, 1967), 366–89, at 370–2, 375. The same consensus is found among recent commentators, see e.g. Wolfgang Schluchter, *Entscheidung für den sozialen Rechtsstaat* (Cologne: Kiepenheuer & Witsch, 1968, repr. Baden-Baden: Nomos, 1983), at 27–32. The difficulties and a corresponding lack of consensus arise when one asks *why* legal science should be seen as having a constitutive function; I pursue the issue below.

[32] See § 11(*b*) of the present text.

[33] See *Phil. Fds.*, at 437. On the basic norm generally, see §§ 27–31(*a*) of the present text. A great many interpretations of the basic norm have been offered in

familiar from the methodological dualism of the Heidelberg neo-Kantians,[34] and, in the guise of the normativity thesis, defended by Kelsen in his Pure Theory. The distinction between 'is' and 'ought' implies altogether separate tracks for establishing, respectively, the truth of empirical claims and, *inter alia*, the validity of legal norms.[35] Kelsen's special concern is of course with the latter. In his view, the validity of a legal norm is established by appeal to the appropriate higher-level norm, whose own validity is established, in turn, by appeal to its higher-level norm, and so on, until the highest level of norms in the legal system is reached, the level of the constitution.[36] An appeal beyond the constitutional level, to a still higher level of positive law norms, is ruled out *ex hypothesi*. And an appeal to matters of fact is precluded by the normativity thesis. A third

the literature, ranging from a Kantian transcendental approach (discussed below), to Alfred Schutz's notion of the basic norm *qua* principle for the construction of ideal-typical interpretive schemes, to Robert Walter's approach in terms of an 'as if' assumption not unlike Vaihinger's. See Alfred Schutz, *The Phenomenology of the Social World* (1st pub. 1932), trans. George Walsh and Frederick Lehnert (Evanston, Ill.: Northwestern UP, 1967), at 246–8; and Robert Walter, 'Der gegenwärtige Stand der Reinen Rechtslehre', *Rechtstheorie*, 1 (1970), 69–95, at 73, 80–3. A rich and wide-ranging statement on the basic norm is Horst Dreier, *Rechtslehre, Staatssoziologie und Demokratietheorie bei Hans Kelsen* (Baden-Baden: Nomos, 1986), at 42–90.

[34] See e.g. Gustav Radbruch, *Legal Philosophy* (1st pub. 1932), trans. Kurt Wilk, in *The Legal Philosophies of Lask, Radbruch, and Dabin*, intro. by Edwin W. Patterson (Cambridge, Mass.: Harvard UP, 1950), 43–224, at 53–9.

[35] Tying the distinction between 'is' and 'ought' to the normativity thesis—in the manner of methodological dualism—is not to deny the familiar distinction between 'is' and 'ought' associated with the separability thesis. On the contrary, Kelsen defends both theses, and the distinction between 'is' and 'ought', systematically ambiguous, reflects his position either on the relation between law and fact or on the relation between law and morality. (See the scheme at p. xxvi.) Where the distinction is invoked on behalf of the normativity thesis, 'ought' flags *legal norms*, and 'is' gives expression to facts; where it is invoked on behalf of the separability thesis, 'ought' flags *norms of morality*, and 'is' gives expression to valid, i.e. existing, legal norms.

[36] See §§ 27–8, 31(a) of the present text. The general idea of tracing back through a normative hierarchy to establish legal validity is familiar; see e.g. James Bryce, *Studies in History and Jurisprudence* (London: Oxford UP, 1901), at 505–6, and H. L. A. Hart, *The Concept of Law* (Oxford: Clarendon Press, 1961), at 103–4. Kelsen traces back through the *Stufenbau*, that is, the hierarchical structure of the legal system as developed by his colleague in the Vienna School, Adolf Julius Merkl. For Merkl's development of the *Stufenbau* doctrine, along with contemporary perspectives on the notion, see *Jurisprudence in Germany and Austria. Selected Modern Themes*, ed. Stanley L. Paulson (Oxford: Clarendon Press, forthcoming).

possible avenue of appeal, that of morality, is closed off by the separability thesis.

How, then, is the validity of norms at the constitutional level to be established? For want of any further appeal, their validity is simply *assumed*. And the assumption takes the form of the basic norm. This reading of the basic norm—or, more precisely, of the intuitive idea giving rise to the basic norm—is evident in one of Kelsen's earliest statements of the 'highest norm' or 'ultimate norm', as he called it then.[37]

If, however, the issue is *why* the norms at the highest level of positive law are valid, then simply to assume that they are valid poses the same question anew. During Kelsen's second and third phases,[38] when Kantian and neo-Kantian elements inform his understanding of the basic norm, he still provides no full statement of the notion. It is a notion that begs for clarification.

The approach I should like to take in an effort to understand the basic norm—and the neo-Kantian underpinnings of Kelsen's theory generally—is to focus on the transcendental argument implicit in the basic norm, where the basic norm is offered as Kelsen's response to the transcendental question. This approach would have Kelsen (i) introducing the notion of normative imputation as his fundamental category, and then (ii) adducing a transcendental or neo-Kantian argument to demonstrate this fundamental category as a presupposition of the data that are given. The basic norm would be relegated to an ancillary role, with references to it amounting simply to allusions to the kind of argument at work. I develop these two points briefly as a sketch of Kelsen's transcendental argument, and then I turn to some details of the transcendental argument and, finally, to an evaluation of how Kelsen fares, thus interpreted.

Kelsen introduces the category of normative imputation by analogy to the category of causation:

Just as laws of nature link a certain material fact as cause with another as effect, so positive laws [in their basic form] link legal condition with legal consequence (the consequence of a so-called unlawful act). If the

---

[37] See Kelsen, 'Reichsgesetz und Landesgesetz nach österreichischer Verfassung', *Archiv des öffentlichen Rechts*, 32 (1914), 202–45, 390–438, at 215–20.

[38] No full periodization of Kelsen's work exists. For what I have in mind here, see the remarks at the outset of the Translators' Preface, above.

mode of linking material facts is causality in the one case, it is imputation in the other . . .[39]

An initial approximation of a transcendental argument, incorporating the category of normative imputation into its second, 'transcendental' premiss, might run as follows:

Argument I

1. One has cognition of legal norms (*given*).
2. Cognition of legal norms is possible only if the category of normative imputation is presupposed (*transcendental premiss*).
3. Therefore, the category of normative imputation is presupposed (*transcendental conclusion*).

Central to Kant's own transcendental argument is the role played by the sceptic. Of equal importance, for the enquiry here, is the distinction between progressive and regressive versions of the transcendental argument. To introduce these notions requires stepping back from the initial approximation of the argument, addressed to Kelsen's theory, and turning to a far more abstract characterization of the argument, in a version that reflects Kant's own enterprise.

Structure of the Transcendental Argument:[40]
The Sceptic's Role, Progressive and Regressive Versions

An abstract characterization of the transcendental argument might begin with a statement '*P*', understood to be true, which, however, can be true only if a further statement, '*Q*', is also true. That is,

---

[39] Kelsen, § 11(*b*) of the present text.

[40] I have drawn on the very considerable literature respecting transcendental arguments, much of it prompted by Peter Strawson's work. See Strawson, *Individuals* (London: Methuen, 1959), at 34–6; and Strawson, *The Bounds of Sense* (London: Methuen, 1966), at 15–32, 72–4, 85–9, *et passim*. For a lucid statement in brief compass, see Ralph C. S. Walker, *Kant* (London: Routledge & Kegan Paul, 1978), at 9–27. See also *Transcendental Arguments and Science*, ed. Peter Bieri *et al.* (Dordrecht: Reidel, 1979); and *Reading Kant*, ed. Eva Schaper and Wilhelm Vossenkuhl (Oxford: Basil Blackwell, 1989). Finally, for a full-dress treatise, see Reinhold Aschenberg, *Sprachanalyse und Transzendentalphilosophie* (Stuttgart: Klett-Cotta, 1982).

Argument II[41]

1. *P.*
2. '*P*' is possible only if *Q*.
3. Therefore *Q*.

In Kant's theory of knowledge, '*P*' stands for the impressions given to consciousness, and '*Q*'—after a number of intermediate steps—for the applicable Kantian category (most obviously, the category of causality). Once '*Q*' is derived (in line 3 of the argument),[42] then—after more intermediate steps—further derivations might be made (demonstrating, in Kantian parlance, the laws of nature as synthetic *a priori* propositions). These further derivations are represented by '*R*' in the sketch of the argument. That is,

4. Therefore *R*.

Kant's argument in the *Critique of Pure Reason* is highlighted in its use as a response to the sceptic, in particular, the sceptical challenge of the philosopher David Hume, and, with respect to normativist legal theory, the anarchist *qua* sceptic suggested by Kelsen himself.[43] The force of Kant's argument, if it is sound, is to show that the sceptic cannot help but undermine his own position in the course of defending it.

Kant's strategy is to set out the steps of the argument in a way designed to trap the sceptic. That is, in the first premiss Kant

[41] The relation between Arguments I and II is set out below; see text at n. 49.

[42] From the standpoint of logical validity, the argument is unproblematic; filled out with a single additional line—1*a*. If *P*, then '*P*' is possible.—the argument proceeds, via the inference rule *modus ponens*, in a perfectly straightforward way to the conclusion at 3. Rather more difficult is the question of the logical status of the premisses, in particular, Kant's own version of line 2. Some writers insist that this premiss has to be analytic, while others contend that it is properly understood as synthetic *a priori*. See e.g. Walker, *Kant* (n. 40 above), at 18–22, defending the former position in reply to a defence of the latter position by T. E. Wilkerson, 'Transcendental Arguments', *Philosophical Quarterly*, 20 (1970), 200–12, and Wilkerson, *Kant's Critique of Pure Reason* (Oxford: Clarendon Press, 1976), at 202–6. Happily, we can ignore this difficult issue here, for I shall be arguing that even if Kant's own version of the transcendental argument is sound, the characteristically neo-Kantian version of the argument is not.

[43] See the text quoted at n. 47 below. While clearly recognizing the anarchist as a sceptic vis-à-vis normativist legal theory, Kelsen is equally clear (as we shall see) in rejecting the suggestion that the Pure Theory might be construed as a reply to the sceptic. Whether anything remains of the regressive version of the transcendental argument once this concession has been made is a question I pursue below.

introduces data that the sceptic will regard as necessary to his own position, but as soon as the sceptic assents to the first premiss, the transition to the applicable Kantian category is inevitable, and the sceptic is caught. While he may have assented quite readily to the first premiss, he would never have dreamt of assenting to the rest of the argument, for it is precisely the Kantian category and, in particular, the further conclusions derived by means of it that have aroused his scepticism. As Ross Harrison neatly puts it, addressing the sceptic's predicament: 'If the sceptic cannot say anything of significance without presupposing the truth of the very thing he was doubting or denying, then he must make a choice between silence and defeat.'[44]

If one key to the structure of the transcendental argument is the role played by the sceptic, another is the distinction, familiar from Kant's *Prolegomena*, between *regressive* and *progressive* versions of the argument.[45] Argument I, above, reflects the regressive version of the transcendental argument, a point to which I shall return. Argument II, above, illustrates the progressive version, reflecting the sort of argument (albeit extremely compressed) that Kant or the Kantian philosopher might develop in the name of the 'transcendental deduction of the categories' in the *Critique of Pure Reason*.[46] The progressive

---

[44] Ross Harrison, 'Wie man dem transzendentalen Ich einen Sinn verleiht', trans. Wolfgang R. Köhler, in *Kants transzendentale Deduktion und die Möglichkeit von Transzendentalphilosophie*, ed. Forum für Philosophie Bad Homburg (Frankfurt: Suhrkamp, 1988), 32–50, at 34–5.

[45] As Kant writes: '[The] analytic method . . . means that one starts from what is being looked for as if it were given, and ascends to the conditions under which alone it is possible. . . . [I]t might be better to call [the analytic method] the *regressive* method in contradistinction to the synthetic or *progressive* method.' *Proleg.* § 5, at p. 31 (note) (Kant's italics). Significantly, Kant uses the subjunctive mood ('as if it were given') in his lines on the so-called regressive method, suggesting that this method is a mere summary formulation of the problem awaiting demonstration by way of the progressive method. The neo-Kantians, on the other hand, take the '*Faktum* of science' as something that is indeed given (see the text quoted at n. 51 below); in contrast to Kant, they are using the regressive method independently of the progressive method.

[46] A cautious approach to Kant's argument might well have one speaking throughout of the 'Kantian philosopher' rather than the historical Kant. For there is neither a consensus on the course of Kant's 'transcendental deduction of the categories', nor, indeed, a detailed understanding of what, in this context, Kant's 18th-century *legal* expression 'deduction' means; on the latter, see Dieter Henrich, 'Kant's Notion of a Deduction and the Methodological Background of the First *Critique*', in *Kant's Transcendental Deductions*, ed. Eckart Förster (Stanford, Calif.: Stanford UP, 1989), at 29–46. My use of Kant's argument,

version begins on a weak note in order to gain the immediate assent of the sceptic, and then proceeds to demonstrate the application of the categories as a condition of the very possibility of experience. The key, as always with the progressive version of the argument, is the role played by the sceptic.

Kelsen and the Progressive Version of the Transcendental Argument

Kelsen makes it abundantly clear that he is not following what I have described as the progressive version of the transcendental argument. As he puts it in the present work:

the Pure Theory is well aware that one cannot prove the existence of the law as one proves the existence of natural material facts and the natural laws governing them, that one cannot adduce compelling arguments to refute a posture like theoretical anarchism, which refuses to see anything but naked power where jurists speak of the law.[47]

A quarter of a century later, Kelsen addresses the same issue and makes the same point:

One can distinguish between lawful and unlawful command acts and objectively interpret interpersonal relations as legal relations, specifically, as legal duties, rights, and powers, *only if* one presupposes the basic norm. Still, this is only one possible interpretation, made possible by the presupposition of the basic norm and dependent on it; it is not a necessary interpretation. Interpersonal relations can also be interpreted as mere power relations, that is, as causes and effects, following the law of causation.[48]

In a word, Kelsen expressly acknowledges the sceptic's position on normativist legal theory as an alternative to his own view. While this acknowledged alternative does not count as another normativist theory of law, it does offer another means of

---

however, turns only on the neo-Kantians' interpretation of it (see n. 42 above); and on this interpretation—namely, that the argument is regressive in character—there is something approaching a consensus (see n. 50 below).

[47] Kelsen, § 16 of the present text; see also § 50(e).

[48] Kelsen, 'On the Basis of Legal Validity' (1st pub. 1960), trans. Stanley L. Paulson, *American Journal of Jurisprudence*, 26 (1981), 178–89, at 185–6 (Kelsen's italics). For other references to Kelsen on the same point, see Raz, *The Authority of Law* (n. 20 above), at 135–8.

rendering coherent the data in question. It is precisely such an alternative, however, that the progressive version of the transcendental argument, if sound, would rule out.

The regressive version of the transcendental argument seems to be better suited, then, to Kelsen's purposes. And, indeed, if one reads Kelsen's theory as drawing its support from the regressive version, one is simply taking one's cues from the neo-Kantian tradition (to which I turn below).

Kelsen and the Regressive Version of the Transcendental Argument

The regressive version of the transcendental argument is illustrated in Argument I, above. It is best understood by contrast with the progressive version, which the Kantian philosopher turns upside down in the regressive version. That is, what was derived in the progressive version of the argument as a secondary conclusion—represented by 'R' in Argument II—is taken as the starting point of the regressive version.

Progressive Version,
Argument II (restated
from above):[49]

1. P (data of consciousness, as given)
2. $\blacklozenge P \supset Q$ (category as condition)
3. Q (category as conclusion)
4. R (statement of cognition, as derived conclusion)———→

Regressive Version,
Argument III (adapted
from Argument I, above):

1. R (statement of cognition, as given)
2. $\blacklozenge R \supset Q$ (category as condition)
3. Q (category as conclusion)

In contrast to the weak starting point of the progressive version,

---

[49] In line 2 of each of the arguments sketched here, the symbol '$\blacklozenge$' stands for the modal operator of possibility; it takes the place of the formulation 'it is possible that'. Similarly in line 2 of each argument, the symbol '$\supset$' takes the place of the formulation 'only if'.

which takes as a given the data of consciousness, the starting point of the regressive version is strong, taking as a given something already known—statement '*R*' as a statement of cognition. The sceptic will not lend his assent here, to be sure, for it is precisely such knowledge claims that are the target of his scepticism. But Kelsen pays no heed, expressly pointing out that he does not mean to answer the sceptic anyway.

The regressive version of the transcendental argument, treated by Kant in his *Prolegomena* as a mere summary statement of the progressive version, emerges as a characteristic mode of argument among the neo-Kantians, not least of all Hermann Cohen, the leading figure of the Marburg School.[50] In a general statement on the Kantian transcendental method, Cohen writes:

If ... I take cognition not as a form and manner of consciousness, but as a *Faktum* that has established itself in *science* and that continues to establish itself *on given foundations*, then the enquiry is no longer directed to a subjective fact; it is directed instead to a fact that, *to whatever extent* self-propagating, is *nevertheless* objectively given, a fact *grounded in principles*. In other words, the enquiry is directed not to the process and apparatus of cognition, but to its result, to science itself. Then the unequivocal question arises: from *which presuppositions* does this fact of science derive its certainty?[51]

[50] I follow the received opinion respecting Cohen's employment of the regressive version of the transcendental argument in his interpretation of Kant. Cohen's use of the regressive version is acknowledged *en passant* by e.g. Rüdiger Bittner, in *Transcendental Arguments and Science* (n. 40 above), at 32, replying to Manfred Baum, ibid., at 1–7; Wolfgang Carl, 'Kant's First Drafts of the Deduction of the Categories', in *Kant's Transcendental Deductions* (n. 46 above), 3–20, at 9–10; and Hans-Georg Gadamer, 'Philosophy or Theory of Science?', in Gadamer, *Reason in the Age of Science*, trans. Frederick G. Lawrence (Cambridge, Mass.: MIT Press, 1981), 151–69, at 151–2. For discussion focused directly on Cohen's use of the regressive version, see Manfred Brelage, *Studien zur Transzendentalphilosophie* (Berlin: de Gruyter, 1965), at 6, 87–8; Manfred Baum, 'Transzendentale Methode', in *Historisches Wörterbuch der Philosophie*, vol. v (Basle: Schwabe, 1980), at 1375–8, repr. in Baum, *Deduktion und Beweis in Kants Transzendentalphilosophie* (Königstein: Athenäum, 1986), at 213–18; Aschenberg, *Transzendentalphilosophie* (n. 40 above), at 367–9; and Geert Edel, *Von der Vernunftkritik zur Erkenntnislogik* (Freiburg: Karl Alber, 1988), 86–8, 100–45. Finally, it should be mentioned that Cohen's interpretation of Kant on this point was followed by the neo-Kantians generally; see e.g. Bruno Bauch, *Wahrheit, Wert und Wirklichkeit* (Leipzig: Felix Meiner, 1923), at 360; and Ernst Cassirer, *The Problem of Knowledge*, trans. William H. Woglom and Charles W. Hendel (New Haven, Conn.: Yale UP, 1950), at 14.

[51] Hermann Cohen, *Das Prinzip der Infinitesimal-Methode und seine Geschichte* (Berlin: Ferd. Dümmler, 1883, repr. Hildesheim: Georg Olms, 1984), 5 (Cohen's italics).

Cohen makes clear, in this and in other statements on Kant's transcendental method,[52] that the argument is to proceed regressively or 'backwards'—from experience that is already cognized, from the *Faktum* of science, to the presupposed category or principle. Kelsen interprets Kant's transcendental method in the same way.[53]

If we follow Kelsen's regressive argument as adumbrated in Argument I, above, we confront questions stemming from the problematic second premiss. There Kelsen claims that the very possibility of cognition of legal norms presupposes the application of a category of normative imputation. But is such a claim even *prima facie* defensible? Is there no other way to anchor a legal philosophy that brings together the normativity thesis and the separability thesis?

To put Kelsen's claim to the test, one can either take a piecemeal approach or appeal to a demonstrative argument. The piecemeal approach, an attempt to anticipate all possible competing theories and then to show that each and every one of them is indefensible, obviously offers no assurance of exhaustiveness. An inventive critic can always come up with still another competing theory—or, what amounts to the same thing, we cannot dismiss this possibility. Exhausting the possibilities requires, instead, a demonstrative argument. Kantians would say, however, that a demonstrative argument, ruling out in one fell swoop all possible alternatives to Kelsen's category of normative imputation, is tantamount to the *progressive* version of the transcendental argument. And—as we have seen—Kelsen did not have in mind a progressive version of the argument.

What is more, if Kelsen were driven to the progressive version, as he now appears to be, he would not fare well. The initial premiss of the progressive version of the transcendental argument must be weak, lest the sceptic withhold his assent to it. More specifically, since the sceptic can easily withhold his assent to any proffered interpretation of experience (he will always have an alternative interpretation), then in order to win his

---

[52] See e.g. Cohen, *Kants Begründung der Ethik* (Berlin: Ferd. Dümmler, 1877), at 24–5 *et passim*; and Cohen, *Kants Theorie der Erfahrung*, 2nd edn. (Berlin: Ferd. Dümmler, 1885), at 77.

[53] See Kelsen, 'Rechtswissenschaft und Recht', *ZöR*, 3 (1922), at 128 *et passim*, repr. in Sander and Kelsen, *Die Rolle des Neukantianismus* (n. 8 above), at 304.

assent, with an eye to trapping him, the initial premiss must record data that are beneath the threshold of interpreted experience. But precisely because the data are beneath the threshold, they will lend themselves to a variety of different interpretations. And—turning now to the legal context—the sceptic will have no compelling reason to assent to a normativist interpretation, much less to a normativist interpretation along the lines suggested by Kelsen.

In a word, the sceptic on normativist legal theory can readily assent to the first premiss of the progressive version of the transcendental argument without being committed thereby to anything more. And then the transcendental argument, designed to 'commit' the sceptic right down the line once assent to the initial premiss is won, must fail.

Thus, Kelsen would face a problem with either version of the transcendental argument. As we have just seen, the progressive version takes as its point of departure a premiss that is simply too weak to be of any help in meeting the sceptic's challenge, rendering this version of the transcendental argument utterly useless to the legal philosopher. The regressive version is more congenial to the legal philosopher, but it claims too much in its second premiss, as though the only way to support a normativist legal theory were by way of the category of imputation. More precisely, the second premiss claims too much *unless* it can be shored up by appealing to the progressive version, which brings us full circle, back to the unworkable progressive version. The conclusion is inescapable: neither version of the transcendental argument works for the legal philosopher.

That Kelsen had no intention of employing the progressive version simply underscores the more general problem here, a problem generated by proceeding as though the regressive version of the argument could be used independently of the progressive version. This independent use of the regressive version of the argument, a move characteristic of the neo-Kantians, robs it of its transcendental force. For the regressive version is promising, in the end, only if it offers a dispositive answer to the sceptic; but it can do that only if it is understood as standing in for a sound transcendental argument in the progressive version. Once the two versions are severed, as in the neo-Kantians' effort to extend the argument to various specific fields,[54] the peculiarly transcendental element is lost, and the regressive version is properly seen as a scheme of analysis.

CONCLUDING REMARKS

I conclude with two brief observations, both prompted by the examination of Kelsen's Kantian argument. First, even if the so-called regressive version of the transcendental argument, severed from the progressive version, collapses into a mere scheme of analysis, it does not follow that Kelsen's Pure Theory of Law collapses with it. Rather, the Pure Theory must simply take its place alongside other normativist legal theories, subjecting itself to the same evaluation they undergo. What will have changed, if the Pure Theory is evaluated in this way, is its claim to uniqueness, its claim to being the only possible normativist legal theory *sans* natural law. This claim—relying as it does on a transcendental argument that cannot be made to work—must be abandoned.

Second, if the Pure Theory takes its place alongside other normativist legal theories, but without the transcendental argument inspired by Kant and the neo-Kantians, it is perhaps best understood as offering a *legal point of view*. This approach, worked out in some detail by Joseph Raz,[55] has affinities to H. L. A. Hart's theory, as well as significant precursors in the two circles most intellectually congenial to Kelsen: the Heidelberg or South-West School of neo-Kantians,[56] and the positivist tradition in German public law.

S. L. P.

---

[54] An example is Georg Simmel, who puts the transcendental question vis-à-vis society, and ties his enquiry to Kant's epistemology (though not, to be sure, without drawing important distinctions); see Simmel, 'How is Society Possible?' (1st pub. 1908), trans. Kurt H. Wolff, in Simmel, *On Individuality and Social Forms. Selected Writings*, ed. Donald N. Levine (Chicago, Ill.: University of Chicago Press, 1971), 6–22.

[55] See Raz, *The Authority of Law* (n. 20 above), at 134–45; and Raz, 'The Purity of the Pure Theory', in *Essays on Kelsen*, ed. Richard Tur and William Twining (Oxford: Clarendon Press, 1986), 79–97.

[56] Kelsen adopted a number of Heidelberg neo-Kantian doctrines, taking over, for example, Wilhelm Windelband's distinction between 'normative' and 'causal' modes of cognition. See *HP*, at 4 *et passim*. Kelsen was not, however, tempted by the peculiarly Heidelberg version of the neo-Kantian argument, a point that emerges fairly clearly from his sharp reply to Heinrich Rickert. See Kelsen, 'Die Rechtswissenschaft als Norm- oder als Kulturwissenschaft', *Schmollers Jahrbuch für Gesetzgebung, Verwaltung und Volkswirtschaft im Deutschen Reich*, 40 (1916), 1181–239, at 1181–207, repr. *WS I*, 37–93, at 37–62.

INTRODUCTION TO THE
PROBLEMS
OF LEGAL THEORY

by
HANS KELSEN

Author's Preface

More than twenty years ago I undertook to develop a pure theory of law, that is, a legal theory purified of all political ideology and every element of the natural sciences, a theory conscious, so to speak, of the autonomy of the object of its enquiry and thereby conscious of its own unique character. Jurisprudence had been almost completely reduced—openly or covertly—to deliberations of legal policy, and my aim from the very beginning was to raise it to the level of a genuine science, a human science. The idea was to develop those tendencies of jurisprudence that focus solely on cognition of the law rather than on the shaping of it, and to bring the results of this cognition as close as possible to the highest values of all science: objectivity and exactitude.

Today I note with some satisfaction that I have not remained alone in pursuing this course. In all the developed countries, I have found heartening approval in every circle of an exceedingly diverse legal profession—theorists and practising lawyers alike —as well as among colleagues in related fields. A number of like-minded individuals have joined together in what is called my 'school', an appropriate label only in the sense that each of us makes an effort to learn from the others without abandoning his own programme. There are also those, not inconsiderable in number, who adopt fundamental positions of the Pure Theory of Law without subscribing to it, sometimes without naming it, indeed even while flatly and less than amiably rejecting it. I am especially grateful to them. For even against their will, they, better than the most faithful followers, bear witness to the usefulness of my theory.

Alongside recognition and imitation, the Pure Theory of Law has prompted an impassioned resistance rarely seen in the history of legal science, a resistance that cannot be explained by the material differences it brings to light. For these differences are based in part on misunderstandings, which, in addition, frequently appear to be less than completely unintentional. Even the real differences that do exist can scarcely justify the great bitterness of my opponents. The besieged Pure Theory is not, after all, so extraordinarily novel, contradicting everything that preceded it. It can be understood as a further development of approaches that emerge in the positivist legal science of the nineteenth century. But my opponents, too, hail from this same positivist legal science. I do not expect today's jurisprudence to change direction completely; rather, I look for a commitment to one of its many directions, an end to its uncertain oscillation.

The uproar in the literature stems less from the novelty of my theory than from its consequences. And this in itself suggests that in the battle against the Pure Theory of Law, sober motives of scientific enquiry are secondary to, above all, political motives—that is, motives highly coloured by the emotions. The question of natural science versus human science cannot be what makes feelings run so high, for the separation of the two has taken place virtually without resistance. It can only be the idea that legal science, a backwoods province far removed from the centre of intellectual activity, accustomed to a slow-paced limp in the direction of progress, is to be moved along a bit more briskly because of direct contact with the general theory of science. Contrary to appearances, the dispute is not in fact about the position of jurisprudence within science, and the consequences of that position. Rather, the dispute is about the relation between legal science and politics, the clean break between them; it is about giving up the deeply rooted custom of making political demands in the name of legal science—the custom, that is, of appealing to an objective authority in representing political demands, which can only be highly subjective, even if they purport in all good faith to be absolute values of a religion, a nation, or a class.

This is the reason why opposition to the Pure Theory of Law borders on hatred, the reason behind the all-out battle against the Pure Theory. The battle touches on the most vital interests of society, and thereby—not least of all—on the professional concerns of the jurist. Understandably, he is reluctant to give up believing and persuading others to believe that, armed with his science, he knows how social conflicts of interest are to be solved 'correctly', that because he understands the law, he is also called upon to shape its content, and that, in his efforts to influence legislation, he is more than a mere 'social technician'—unlike other politicians.

The required separation of legal science from politics does have political consequences, negative ones, and it is understandable that opponents are hardly inclined to be fair to a theory that calls on legal science to exercise this self-restraint, which many regard as self-demotion. In order to be able to resist such a theory, its opponents must disallow its true nature. The arguments that are directed, then, not really against the Pure Theory of Law but against a phantom of it, adapted to the needs of its opponents of the moment, cancel each other out, rendering a rebuttal almost superfluous. Some say contemptuously that the Pure Theory is completely lacking in content, that it is an empty game of hollow concepts. Others warn that the substance of the Pure Theory, because of its subversive tendencies, poses a serious threat to the existing state and its law. One of the objections most frequently raised against the Pure Theory is that by remaining entirely free of all politics, it stands apart from the ebb and flow of life and is therefore worthless in terms of science. No less frequently, however, it is said that the Pure Theory of Law is not in a position to fulfil its own basic methodological requirement, and is itself merely the expression of a certain political value. But which political value? Fascists declare that the Pure Theory is on the side of democratic liberalism, while liberal or social democrats regard it as a trail-blazer for Fascism. Communists write off the Pure Theory as the ideology of capitalistic statism, while nationalists and capitalists write it off sometimes as Bolshevism, sometimes as covert anarchism. There are those who assure us that the Pure Theory is intellectually related to Catholic scholasticism, and others who believe that it has the characteristics of Protestant political and legal theory. And there are even those who would like to brand it as atheistic. In a word, the Pure Theory of Law has been suspected of every single political persuasion there is. Nothing could attest better to its purity.

If there is to be such a thing as a science of law at all, the methodological postulate of purity cannot be seriously questioned. Doubts could only be entertained about the extent to which the postulate can be fulfilled. One must be sure to take into account that on precisely this point, natural science and the social sciences differ considerably. Not that natural science is spared the danger that political interests will attempt to wield influence over it; history demonstrates otherwise, and shows clearly enough that even the truth about the movement of the stars might well cause a world power to feel threatened. If natural science has succeeded, by and large, in asserting its independence from politics, the reason is that this victory has served a social interest more powerful than politics: the interest in technological progress, which independent research alone can guarantee. But there is no path so immediately clear, leading so directly from social theory to social progress, that is, to the indisputable advantages guaranteed by progress in terms of social technique, there is no path comparable to the one leading from physics and chemistry to the triumphs of mechanical engineering and medical therapy. The social sciences—not least of all because they are undeveloped—are still lacking in a social power that could oppose the overwhelming interest of rulers (as well as rulers-in-waiting) in a theory tailored to their wishes, that is, in social ideology. This is all the more so in our own time, reeling from the World War and its consequences, a time in which the very foundations of social life have been profoundly shaken, exacerbating in the extreme the tensions between states as well as within states. The absolute value of an objective science of law and politics has prospects of general recognition only in a period of social stability. And so nothing seems less opportune today than a theory of law that aims to maintain its purity at a time when other theories are willing to offer themselves up to any and all powers, when one no longer shrinks from calling loudly and publicly for a legal science that is political and then claiming that it is 'pure'—thus extolling as virtue what only the most acute personal exigencies could barely excuse.

If I nevertheless venture to bring together at this time the results of my earlier work on the problem of law, I do so in the hope that those who place intellectual values before power are more numerous than it presently seems. And I do so, above all, in the hope that a younger generation, caught in the raucous hue and cry of our times, will not abandon altogether the belief in a free and independent legal science. For it is my firm conviction that in some distant future, the fruits of such a legal science will not be lost.

Hans Kelsen
Geneva
May 1934

I

Law and Nature

§ 1. 'Purity'

The Pure Theory of Law is a theory of positive law, of positive law as such, and not of any special system of law. It is general legal theory, not an interpretation of particular national or international legal norms.

As theory, the Pure Theory of Law aims solely at cognition of its subject-matter, its object. It attempts to answer the questions of what the law is and how the law is made, not the questions of what the law ought to be or how the law ought to be made. The Pure Theory of Law is legal science,[1] not legal policy.[2]

It characterizes itself as a 'pure' theory of law because it aims at cognition focused on the law alone, and because it aims to eliminate from this cognition everything not belonging to the object of cognition, precisely specified as the law. That is, the Pure Theory aims to free legal science of all foreign elements. This is its basic methodological principle. The principle may appear obvious, but a glance at traditional legal science as it has developed in the nineteenth and twentieth centuries shows clearly just how far the tradition is from meeting the requirement of purity. In an utterly uncritical way, jurisprudence[3] has been

---

[1] 'legal science' ('Rechtswissenschaft'). On the distinction between 'legal science', 'legal theory', and related expressions, see Supplementary Note 1, in appendix I; see also n. 3 below.

[2] 'legal policy' ('Rechtspolitik'). Comparable to 'foreign policy', 'monetary policy', and the like, 'legal policy' refers generally to the various considerations—of both means and ends—that bear on the question of what ought to be enacted as law. For some details, see Supplementary Note 2, in appendix I.

[3] In the course of this paragraph, Kelsen uses three different expressions—'jurisprudence' ('Jurisprudenz'), 'legal scholar' ('Rechtsgelehrte'), and 'legal science' ('Rechtswissenschaft')—to refer to one and the same enterprise, namely, academic enquiry into positive law. For some details on this and related nomenclature, see Supplementary Note 1, in appendix I.

entangled in psychology and biology, in ethics and theology. Today the legal scholar regards almost no specialized field of enquiry as beyond his purview. Indeed, he believes that it is precisely by borrowing from other disciplines that he can enhance his scholarly reputation. The result, of course, is that legal science as such is lost.

§ 2. Natural Material Fact (Act) and Meaning

The Pure Theory of Law seeks to delimit clearly the object of its cognition. The independence of this object is threatened from two directions by the prevailing methodological syncretism alluded to above, and the Pure Theory takes both into account.[4] Law is a social phenomenon, that is, observable in society; and society as an object of enquiry is completely different from nature, for it comprises a completely different network of elements. If legal science is not to merge into the natural sciences, the law must be contrasted with nature as sharply as possible. And this is especially difficult to do since at least part of the essence of the law (or what at first blush is usually referred to as law) appears to occupy the realm of nature, to have a thoroughly natural existence. If one analyses a parliamentary enactment, say, or an administrative act, a judicial decision, a private law transaction, a delict—all of which are referred to as [belonging to the] law—one can distinguish two elements. There is an act perceptible to the senses, taking place in time and space, an external event, usually an instance of human behaviour. And there is a specific meaning, a sense that is, so to speak, immanent in or attached to the act or event. People assemble in a hall, they give speeches, some rise, others remain seated—this is the external event. Its meaning: that a statute is enacted. Or, a man dressed in robes says certain words from a platform, addressing someone standing before him. This external event has as its meaning a judicial decision. A merchant writes a certain letter to another merchant, who writes back in reply. This means they have entered into a contract. An individual somehow acts to

---

[4] See § 1 for Kelsen's allusion to entanglements in psychology and biology on the one hand, in ethics and theology on the other. On methodological syncretism, see also n. 14 of the Introduction, above.

bring about the death of another, and this means, legally speaking, murder.

§ 3. Self-Interpretation of Social Data (Subjective and Objective Meaning)

This 'meaning' is not something one can see or hear in the act *qua* external material fact, as one can perceive in an object its natural properties and functions, such as colour, rigidity, and weight. But the act itself (if it expresses itself verbally) can say something about its meaning, can declare its own sense. Indeed, this is a characteristic unique to the data of social and, in particular, legal cognition. A plant cannot say anything about itself to the botanist. It makes no attempt to explain itself in terms of the natural sciences. A social act, however, may very well carry with it a self-interpretation, a statement about what it means, for the acting individual himself attaches to his act a certain sense, which is expressed in some way or another and which is understood by those to whom the act is addressed. People assembled in a parliament can expressly declare their intention to enact a statute; two private parties can state their intention to enter into a legal transaction. Cognition encompassing the law usually discovers a self-interpretation of data that anticipates the interpretation to be provided by legal science.

It is necessary, then, to distinguish between the subjective and the objective meaning of an act. The subjective meaning may, but need not, coincide with the objective meaning attributed to the act in the system of all legal acts, that is, the legal system. The act of the famous Captain from Köpenick[5] was to have been— its subjective meaning—an administrative directive. Objectively, however, it was not an administrative directive but a delict. When members of a secret society, intending to rid their country of undesirables, condemn to death someone they regard as a traitor, they themselves consider their act, subjectively, to be a

---

[5] In 1906, a shoemaker, Wilhelm Voigt, donned the uniform of a captain of the guard, and, with the help of several unsuspecting soldiers, occupied the city hall at Köpenick (near Berlin), arrested the mayor, and seized the city treasury. Kelsen's references to the episode go back at least as far as 1913. It is best known, however, as the point of departure for Carl Zuckmayer's highly successful comedy, *Der Hauptmann von Köpenick* (1931).

pronouncement of the death penalty. They call it that, and instruct their agent to kill the condemned party. Objectively—in the system of objective law—the killing is murder by secret tribunal, and not the carrying-out of a death penalty. And this is so even though the external circumstances of the act cannot be distinguished from those of carrying out a death penalty.

§ 4. The Norm as Scheme of Interpretation

These external circumstances are always a part of nature, for they are events perceptible to the senses, taking place in time and space; and, as a part of nature, they are governed by causal laws. As elements of the system of nature, these events as such are not objects of specifically legal cognition, and thus are not legal in character at all. What makes such an event a legal (or an illegal) act is not its facticity, not its being natural, that is, governed by causal laws and included in the system of nature. Rather, what makes such an event a legal act is its meaning, the objective sense that attaches to the act. The specifically legal sense of the event in question, its own peculiarly legal meaning, comes by way of a norm whose content refers to the event and confers legal meaning on it; the act can be interpreted, then, according to this norm. The norm functions as a scheme of interpretation. The norm is itself created by way of a legal act whose own meaning comes, in turn, from another norm. That a material fact is not murder but the carrying-out of a death penalty is a quality, imperceptible to the senses, that first emerges by way of an act of intellect, namely, confrontation with the criminal code and with criminal procedure. The aforementioned exchange of letters[6] means that a contract has been concluded, and it has this meaning solely because these circumstances fall under certain provisions of the civil code. That an assembly of people is a parliament, and that the result of their activity is a statute (in other words, that these events have this 'meaning'), says simply that the material facts as a whole correspond to certain provisions of the constitution. That is, the content of an actual event corresponds to the content of a given norm.

[6] See § 2.

§ 5. The Norm as Act and as Meaning[7]

It is to these norms that legal cognition is directed—norms that confer on certain material facts the character of legal (or illegal) acts, and that are themselves created by way of such legal acts. One should note here that the norm *qua* specific meaning is something other than the mental act of intending or imagining the norm. Intending or imagining the norm must be kept clearly separate from the norm somehow intended or imagined. To speak of the 'creation' of a norm always has reference to those material events that carry, as it were, the norm *qua* meaning. The Pure Theory of Law does not look to mental processes or physical events of any kind in seeking to cognize norms, in seeking to comprehend something legally. To comprehend something legally can only be to comprehend it as law. The thesis that only legal norms can be the object of legal cognition is a tautology, for the law—the sole object of legal cognition—is norm,[8] and norm is a category[9] that has no application in the realm of nature. To characterize acts occurring in nature as legal is simply to claim the validity of norms whose content corresponds in a certain way to that of actual events. When a judge establishes as a given a concrete material fact (say, a delict), his cognition is directed first of all simply to something existing in nature. His cognition becomes legal at the point at which he brings together the material fact he has established and the statute he is to apply; that is to say, his cognition becomes legal when he interprets the material fact as 'theft' or 'fraud'. And this interpretation is possible only if the content of the material fact is cognized in a very specific way, namely, as the content of a norm. (One should note here that the activity of the judge is by no means exhausted in the act of cognition, which is

---

[7] 'Meaning' (here, and occasionally elsewhere, '*Sinngehalt*'). The German, read literally, is 'meaning-content'. See e.g. §§ 14(*c*)–15.

[8] 'the law is norm' ('*das Recht ist Norm*'). Kelsen uses this cryptic expression to allude to the law in making the distinction between the natural and the ideal, between causal law and norm. In each instance, the law tracks the latter of the paired concepts. See e.g. §§ 7, 8, 11(*a*), 15, 19, 29.

[9] 'category' ('*Kategorie*'). Following, *inter alia*, Georg Simmel, Kelsen often uses the term to refer to irreducible kinds—in Simmel's scheme, norm, being, and idea. See Simmel, *Einleitung in die Moralwissenschaft*, vol. i (Berlin: Wilhelm Hertz, 1892, repr. Aalen: Scientia, 1983), 8–13, and cp. *HP*, 7 f. *et passim*.

simply preparation for the act of will whereby the individual norm[10] of the judicial decision is issued.)

§ 6. Validity and Sphere of Validity of the Norm

To speak, as above,[11] of the 'validity' of a norm is to express first of all simply the specific existence of the norm, the particular way in which the norm is given, in contradistinction to natural reality, existing in space and time. The norm as such, not to be confused with the act by means of which the norm is issued, does not exist in space and time, for it is not a fact of nature. The possible content of the norm, however, is the same as the possible content of an actual event, for the norm refers in its content to this actual event, above all, to human behaviour. The norm must, then, also determine in its content both where and when the behaviour takes place—or, in terms of the norm, 'ought to take place'. The validity of norms governing human behaviour generally (and so, the validity of legal norms in particular) is spatial and temporal validity because these norms have as their content spatial and temporal events. That a norm is valid will always mean that it is valid in some space or another and for some time or another—in other words, that it refers to events that can only take place somewhere and at some time.

The connection of the norm to space and time is its spatial and temporal sphere of validity. While this sphere of validity may be limited, it may also be unlimited. The norm may be valid only for a certain space and time, determined by itself or by another norm; that is, it may govern only those events that occur within a certain space and time. Or, the norm may be valid—according to its meaning—everywhere and always; that is to say, the norm may refer to events wherever and whenever it is possible for them to occur. And this will be the meaning of a norm that contains no particular determination of space and time. It is not that the norm is then valid apart from space and time, but that space and time are indeterminate; the spatial and temporal sphere of validity of the norm is unlimited.

---

[10] 'individual norm' ('*individuelle Norm*'). Kelsen uses the term to refer to the individualized norm, the concretization of the general norm. See e.g. § 31(*b*)–(*e*).
[11] See § 5.

In addition to the spatial and temporal sphere of validity, one can distinguish an objective (or a material) sphere of the validity of norms by considering the particular objects, the various forms of human behaviour, that are normatively regulated—such as religious, economic, political behaviour, and so on. And if one asks about the human beings whose behaviour is being regulated, one can also distinguish norms in terms of a personal sphere of validity. The material sphere of validity may be unlimited or limited, in the sense that a certain norm, to be created in a certain way and belonging to a certain system, may refer in its content to any object whatsoever or, alternatively, only to particular objects—as, for example, where a federal constitution divides the material sphere of validity between the norms of the federal system and those of the member-state systems. The personal sphere of validity, too, may be unlimited or limited. The norms of a universal morality are addressed to absolutely all human beings; that is, these norms have in principle an unlimited personal sphere of validity. And there are legal norms that impose obligations on, and grant rights to, certain categories of human beings; that is, these norms have only a limited personal sphere of validity.

§ 7. Cognition of Legal Norms vs. Legal Sociology

In characterizing the law as norm, and in restricting legal science to the cognition of norms (a function different from both making and applying the law), one separates the law from nature, one separates legal science as a cognitive science of norms from all those cognitive sciences that aim to explain natural events in terms of causal laws. One even separates legal science from a cognitive science whose task is to enquire into the causes and effects of those natural events that, interpreted by way of legal norms, are represented as legal acts. There is no objection to characterizing such research as sociology—in particular, legal sociology. As for its prospects and its value, nothing further need be said here. Only this might be pointed out: cognition in legal sociology is not concerned with the legal norm *qua* specific meaning; rather, it is directed to certain events quite apart from their connection to norms that are recognized or presupposed as valid. Legal sociology does not relate the material facts in question to valid norms; rather, it relates these material facts to still other material facts as causes and effects. It asks, say, what prompts a legislator to decide on exactly these norms and to issue no others, and it asks what effects his regulations have had. It asks how religious imagination, say, or economic data influence the activity of the courts, and what motivates people to behave or to fail to behave in conformity with the legal system. The law comes into question in enquiries of this sort only as a material datum, as a fact in the consciousness of those human beings issuing legal norms or complying with and violating them. The object of such cognition, then, is not actually the law itself, but certain parallel phenomena in nature. Similarly with the physiologist: he investigates the chemical or physical processes that accompany certain feelings or give rise to conditions under which these feelings occur, but he does not comprehend the feelings themselves, which, as psychological phenomena, cannot be comprehended chemically or physiologically. The Pure Theory of Law, as a specifically legal science, directs its attention not to legal norms as the data of consciousness, and not to the intending or imagining of legal norms either, but rather to legal norms *qua* (intended or imagined) meaning. And the Pure Theory encompasses material facts only where these facts are the content of legal norms, that is, are governed by legal norms. The problem of the Pure Theory of Law is the specific autonomy of a realm of meaning.

II

Law and Morality

§ 8. Law and Justice

In marking off the law from nature, the Pure Theory of Law
seeks the boundary between the natural and the ideal.[12] Legal
science belongs not to the natural sciences, but to the human
sciences.[13] One can argue over whether the opposition between
the natural and the ideal coincides with the opposition between
natural reality and value, between 'is' and 'ought', between
causal law and norm, or whether the realm of the ideal is indeed
broader than the realm of value, of 'ought', of norm. One will
not be able to deny, however, that the law *qua* norm is an ideal
reality, not a natural reality. And with that the task is set: just as
one distinguishes the law from nature, so one is also to
distinguish the ideal phenomenon, law, from other ideal
phenomena, especially from norms of other types. Here, above
all, the task is to unfetter the law, to break the connection that is
always made between the law and morality. What is rejected
thereby is not, of course, the dictate that the law ought to be
moral and good; that goes without saying, though what it really
means is another question. Rather, what is rejected is simply the
view that the law as such is part of morality, and that therefore
every law, as law, is in some sense and to some degree moral.
Depicting the law as a branch of morality may simply amount to
the obvious dictate that the law ought to be shaped in
accordance with morality, or it may mean that the law as a part
of morality actually has moral character. Either way, it is an

[12] 'Ideal' ('*Geist*') reflects Kelsen's and Wilhelm Windelband's usage, jux-
taposing the natural and the ideal generally. See Supplementary Note 3, in
appendix I.

[13] 'human sciences' ('*Geisteswissenschaften*'). The expression covers the fields
brought together, roughly speaking, under the rubric of the humanities. For some
details on this nomenclature, see Supplementary Note 3, in appendix I.

attempt to confer upon the law the absolute value claimed by morality.

The law as a moral category is tantamount to justice, the expression used for a social ordering that is absolutely right, that fully achieves its objective by satisfying everyone. The longing for justice, considered psychologically, is the eternal longing of man for happiness, which he cannot find as an individual and therefore seeks in society. Social happiness is called 'justice'.

The word 'justice', to be sure, is also used in a legal sense, in terms of conformity to positive law—in particular, conformity to statute. That a general norm is applied in one case but not in a similarly situated case appears, then, as 'unjust'; and it appears 'unjust' quite apart from any consideration of the value of the general norm itself. According to this usage, judging something to be just is simply to express the relative value of conformity to a norm; 'just' is simply another word for 'right'.

In its literal meaning, however, different from this legal sense of the word, 'justice' stands for an absolute value. Its content cannot be determined by the Pure Theory of Law or, indeed, arrived at by way of rational cognition at all—as the history of human intellectual endeavour demonstrates, with its failure over a millennium to resolve this problem. For in its absolute validity, justice, which must be imagined as an order different from, and higher than, the positive law, lies as much beyond all experience as the Platonic idea lies beyond natural reality, and the transcendent thing-in-itself lies beyond appearances. The dualism of law and justice has the same metaphysical character as this ontological dualism. And, like ontological dualism, the dualism of law and justice also has a double capacity, that is, its function depends on whether its bias is optimistic or pessimistic, conservative or revolutionary: on one occasion it affirms what exists—the system of the state or of society—as being in agreement with the absolute value,[14] on another occasion it disavows what exists as standing in contradiction to that value.

---

[14] 'Absolute value', our rendition here and occasionally elsewhere of the German 'Ideal' (see e.g. Kelsen's Preface, at p. 2), avoids confusion with 'ideal', our rendition of the German 'Geist', which is contrasted with 'natural' at the outset of the present section (see also n. 12 above, and Supplementary Note 3, in appendix I). 'Absolute value' ('absoluter Wert') is one of several expressions used by Kelsen himself to refer to the absolute qua highest standard or ideal (see e.g. the first sentence of the present paragraph).

And just as it is impossible, in keeping with the very presupposition, to fix the essence of the Platonic idea or of the thing-in-itself
in rational cognition oriented to experience, so also it is
impossible to answer in that way the question of what justice is.
Until now, all attempts along these lines have led to completely
empty formulas, such as: 'do good and avoid evil', 'to each his
own', 'hold to the golden mean', and the like. Even the
categorical imperative is entirely without content. If one turns to
cognitive science for a determination of the absolute value
designated by 'ought', one learns only that you ought to do what
you ought to do. Behind this tautology lurks the logical principle of
identity, in multifarious forms and painstaking disguise, the
insight that the good is good and not evil, that the just is just and
not unjust, and that A is the same as A and not the same as not-A.
An absolute value of will and of action, justice made into an
object of cognition must transform itself all of a sudden into the
idea of truth that is expressed (negatively) in the principle of
identity. This denaturing of the problem is the inevitable result of
forcing into a logical scheme an object that is at bottom alien to
logic.

   Seen from the standpoint of rational cognition, there are only
interests and thus conflicts of interests, which are resolved by
way of an ordering of interests that either satisfies the one at the
expense of the other, or establishes a balance, a compromise
between the opposing interests. That only one ordering of
interests has absolute value (which really means, 'is just') cannot
be accounted for by way of rational cognition. If there were
justice in the sense in which one usually appeals to it when one
wants to assert certain interests over others, then the positive law
would be completely superfluous, its existence entirely incom-
prehensible. Given an absolutely good social order emerging
from nature, reason, or divine will, the activity of the legislator
would be as foolish as artificial illumination in the brightest
sunlight. The usual objection, however, is that although there is
indeed justice, we cannot define it, or, what amounts to the same
thing, we cannot define it unequivocally. This objection is a
contradiction in terms, masking in typically ideological fashion
the all too painful truth: justice *qua* absolute value is irrational.
However indispensable it may be for human will and action, it is
not accessible to cognition. Only positive law is given to

cognition, or, more accurately, is given to cognition as a task.[15]
The less one strives to separate clearly the positive law from
justice, and the more indulgent one is toward the lawmaker's
efforts to have the law also accepted somehow as just, the more
one lends support to the ideological bias that is characteristic of
classical, conservative natural law theory. What matters there is
less the cognition of prevailing law than a justification of it, a
transfiguration, achieved by showing that the positive law is
simply the emanation of a natural or divine order or of a system
of reason—the emanation of an absolutely 'right', just order.
Revolutionary natural law theory, which has played a relatively
modest role in the history of legal science, has the opposite
intention, that of calling into question the validity of the positive
law by claiming that the positive law contradicts some presupposed absolute order. So it is that revolutionary natural law
theory sometimes represents the reality of the law in a more
unfavourable light than the truth warrants.

§ 9. Anti-Ideological Stance of the Pure Theory of Law

These ideological biases, with obvious designs or effects in terms
of power politics, still dominate legal science, notwithstanding
the apparent demise of the natural law theory. The Pure Theory
of Law is directed against them. The Pure Theory aims to depict
the law as it is, without legitimizing it as just or disqualifying it
as unjust; the Pure Theory enquires into actual and possible law,
not into 'right' law. In this sense, it is a radically realistic legal
theory. It refuses to evaluate the positive law. To grasp the
positive law in its essence, and to understand the positive law by
analysing its structure—this alone is the task the Pure Theory of
Law sets for itself as a cognitive science. In particular, the Pure
Theory refuses to serve political interests of one sort or another
by providing the ideological means either to legitimize or to
disqualify the existing social order. It thereby stands in sharpest
opposition to traditional legal science, which is wittingly or
unwittingly ideological in character, sometimes more so, some-

---

[15] 'given to cognition as a task' ('*dem Erkennen aufgegeben*'). Cp. e.g. *CPR*,
at A498–500/B526–8.

times less. Precisely through its anti-ideological stance, the Pure Theory of Law proves itself as a true legal science, whose immanent aspiration is the unveiling of the object of its cognition. Ideology veils reality by transfiguring it, with the aim of conserving, defending it; or ideology veils reality by distorting it, with the aim of attacking, destroying it, and replacing it with another reality. All ideology has its roots in will, not in cognition; ideology stems from certain interests, or, more correctly, from interests other than the interest in truth. (Nothing is being said hereby, of course, about the value or virtue of these other interests.) Again and again cognition rends the veil that the will, through ideology, draws over things. The authority who creates the law, and thus seeks to preserve it, may ask whether an ideologically free cognition of his product is useful. And even the forces that aim to destroy the existing system and replace it with another, deemed to be better, may not know what to make of legal cognition that is free of ideology. Nevertheless, a cognitive science of the law cannot concern itself with either the authority who would preserve the system or the forces that would destroy it. And a cognitive science of the law is what the Pure Theory of Law aims to be.

III

The Concept of Law and the Doctrine of the Reconstructed Legal Norm

§ 10. Natural Law Theory and Legal Positivism

The ideological character of traditional legal theory, the theory assailed by the Pure Theory of Law, is apparent in the familiar definition of the concept of law. Traditional theory even today is under the influence of conservative natural law theory, with, as mentioned above, its transcendent concept of law.[16] This concept corresponds completely to the metaphysical character of philosophy during the period in which natural law theory prevailed, a period coinciding politically with the emergence of the police state of the absolute monarchy. The victory of the liberal bourgeoisie in the nineteenth century was the beginning of an outspoken reaction against metaphysics and natural law theory. Hand in hand with progress in the empirical natural sciences and with the breakdown of religious ideology, bourgeois legal science shifted from natural law to legal positivism. Still, however radical this shift may have been, it never amounted to an about-face. To be sure, the law is no longer presupposed as an eternal and absolute category; its content is recognized as subject to historical change, and the law itself, as positive law, is recognized as a phenomenon conditioned by temporal and spatial factors. The notion of an absolute legal value, however, is not completely lost, living on in an idea cherished even in positivist jurisprudence, namely, the ethical idea of justice. Even where the distinction between law and justice is emphatically

---

[16] Kelsen alludes here and above, at § 8, to a 'transcendent' concept, going beyond the limits of experience, by contrast with the distinctively Kantian 'transcendental' concept, which marks the enquiry into the conditions of possible experience. See, on the latter, §§ 11(b)–(c), 29.

drawn, the two nevertheless remain bound together by more or less visible ties. In order to be 'law', so theory has it, the positive state system must have some concern for justice, be it a matter of assuring an ethical minimum,[17] be it a matter of attempting, however inadequately, to be 'right' law, that is, simply, to be just. In order to be 'law', the positive law must correspond in some measure, however modest, to the idea of law,[18] to justice. Since the legal character of the prevailing state system is presupposed as self-evident, no more is required to legitimize the system than this legal theory of the moral minimum, simply a natural law theory writ small. And this minimal guarantee suffices in those comparatively quiet times when a consolidated bourgeoisie is in power, as well as in periods of a relative balance of power among the various social factions. The ultimate conclusions of the officially recognized positivist principle are not drawn, then, and legal science is not completely positivistic in orientation. It is, however, preponderantly positivistic.

§ 11. 'Ought' as Designating a Category of the Law

(a) 'Ought' as Designating a Transcendent Idea

The orientation of legal science described above is expressed clearly in the concept subsuming the positive law, the concept of norm or 'ought'. While the non-identity of legal and moral norms is stressed again and again in jurisprudence, an absolute moral value is not called into question. It may simply be that an absolute moral value goes unchallenged so that the merely relative value of the law might stand out all the more clearly against this background. Nevertheless, the mere fact that jurisprudence does not deny the existence of an absolute value, does not consider itself competent to pass on the question, is a fact that must have repercussions for the concept of law. Indeed,

---

[17] The allusion is to Georg Jellinek's doctrine that 'the law is nothing other than the *ethical minimum*', in Jellinek, *Die sozialethische Bedeutung von Recht, Unrecht und Strafe* (Vienna: Alfred Hölder, 1878, repr. Hildesheim: Georg Olms, 1967), 42 (Jellinek's emphasis).

[18] 'idea of law' ('*Rechtsidee*'). The term is familiar in the German-language literature as a label for justice, understood as the peculiarly legal value. For some details and text references, see Supplementary Note 4, in appendix I.

if the law is viewed as norm, just as morality is, and if the meaning of the legal norm is expressed in an 'ought', just as that of the moral norm is, then something of the absolute value that is characteristic of morality does attach to the concept of the legal norm and to the legal 'ought'. The judgment that something is legally regulated, that some [norm-]content is obligatory owing to the law, is never entirely free of the notion that for this to be so is good, right, and just. And in this sense, the conceptual characterization of the law as norm and as 'ought', offered by the positivist jurisprudence of the nineteenth century, does in fact retain a certain ideological element.

(b) 'Ought' as Designating a Transcendental Category

The Pure Theory of Law seeks to free the conceptual characterization of the law from this ideological element by completely severing the concept of the legal norm from its source, the concept of the moral norm, and by securing the autonomy of the law even vis-à-vis the moral law. The Pure Theory does this not by understanding the legal norm, like the moral norm, as an imperative—the usual approach of traditional theory—but by understanding the legal norm as a hypothetical judgment[19] that expresses the specific linking of a conditioning material fact with a conditioned consequence. The legal norm becomes the reconstructed legal norm,[20] which exhibits the basic form of positive laws.[21] Just as laws of nature link a certain material fact as cause with another as effect, so positive laws [in their basic form] link legal condition with legal consequence (the consequence of a so-called unlawful act). If the mode of linking material facts is causality in the one case, it is imputation in the other, and imputation is recognized in the Pure Theory of Law as the particular lawfulness, the autonomy, of the law.[22] Just as an

---

[19] 'hypothetical judgment' ('hypothetisches Urteil').

[20] 'reconstructed legal norm' ('Rechtssatz'). The expression is Eugenio Bulygin's terminology for Kelsen's hypothetically formulated legal norm as introduced in the present section. See also § 29, text at n. 42. For some details, see Supplementary Note 5, in appendix I.

[21] 'basic form of positive laws' ('Grundform des Gesetzes'). Cp. e.g. 'reconstructed legal norm' (see n. 20 above), 'legal norm in its primary form' (see § 14(b), text at n. 25), and 'the concept of statutory form' (see § 31(b), text at n. 51).

[22] 'imputation' ('Zurechnung'). Kelsen distinguishes between so-called

effect is traced back to its cause, so a legal consequence is traced back to its legal condition. The legal consequence, however, cannot be regarded as having been caused by the legal condition. Rather, the legal consequence (the consequence of an unlawful act) is linked by imputation to the legal condition. That is what it means to say that someone is punished 'because' of a delict, that a lien against someone's property is executed 'because' of an unpaid debt. The connection of the punishment to the delict, of the execution of the lien to the material fact of an unlawful civil act, has normative import, not causal import. Expressing this connection, termed 'imputation', and thereby expressing the specific existence, the validity, of the law—and nothing else—is the 'ought' in which the Pure Theory of Law represents the positive law. That is, 'ought' expresses the unique sense in which the material facts belonging to the system of the law are posited in their reciprocal relation. In the same way, 'must' expresses the law of causality.

Both cases involve simply the expression of a functional connection of elements, the connection specific to the respective system—here nature, there the law. In particular, even causality represents only a functional connection when one frees it of the metaphysico-magical sense originally attached to it by man, still entirely animistic and imagining in the cause some secret force creating, out of itself, the effect. A causal principle thus purified can never be dispensed with in the natural sciences, for what is manifest in the principle is simply the postulate of the intelligibility of nature, a postulate that can be approximated only by linking the material facts given to our cognition. Laws of nature say: 'if A is, then B must be.' Positive laws say: 'if A is, then B ought to be.' And neither the laws of nature nor positive laws have said anything thereby about the moral or political value of the connection between A and B. The 'ought' designates a relative *a priori* category[23] for comprehending empirical legal

peripheral imputation (addressed in the present section) and central imputation (addressed at § 25(a), (d)). On the distinction generally, and on 'imputation' as the English-language rendering of '*Zurechnung*', see Supplementary Note 6, in appendix I.

[23] 'a relative *a priori* category' ('*eine relativ apriorische Kategorie*'), rendering '*relativ*' as an adjective. See e.g. Kelsen, *Das Problem der Souveränität* (Tübingen: J. C. B. Mohr, 1920, repr. Aalen: Scientia, 1960), at p. viii; and Felix Somló, *Juristische Grundlehre* (Leipzig: Felix Meiner, 1917, repr. Aalen: Scientia, 1973), at 127.

data. In this respect, the 'ought' is indispensable, lest the specific way in which the positive law connects material facts with one another not be comprehended or expressed at all. For it is obvious that this connection is not the connection of cause and effect. It is not as the effect of a cause that punishment is set for a delict; rather, the legislator establishes between these two material facts, delict and punishment, a linkage that is completely different from causality. Completely different, but just as inviolable. For in the system of the law, that is, owing to the law, punishment follows always and without exception from the delict, even if, in the system of nature, punishment may fail to materialize for one reason or another. Where punishment does materialize, it need not occur as an effect of the delict, functioning as cause; it can have entirely different causes, even if, indeed, the delict has not taken place at all. When one says that if a so-called unlawful act occurs, the consequence of the unlawful act 'ought' to occur, this 'ought'—as designating a category of the law—simply represents the specific sense in which legal condition and legal consequence belong together in the reconstructed legal norm. This category of the law has a purely formal character, which distinguishes it in principle from a transcendent idea of law. It remains applicable whatever the content of the material facts so linked, and whatever the type of the acts to be understood as law. No social reality can be excluded, on the basis of its content, from this legal category, which is cognitively and theoretically transcendental in terms of the Kantian philosophy, not metaphysically transcendent. Precisely its transcendental character serves to preserve its radically anti-ideological stance; and on precisely this point, traditional legal theory launches the fiercest resistance, finding it intolerable that the system of the Soviet Union is to be conceived of as a legal system in exactly the same way as is that of Fascist Italy or democratic, capitalistic France.

(c) *Regress to Natural Law and Metaphysics*

The social convulsions caused by the World War have primed traditional legal theory for a wholesale return to natural law, even as traditional philosophy adopts a posture of complete regress to pre-Kantian metaphysics. The bourgeoisie near the midpoint of the twentieth century, in the same political situation

as the feudal lord at the beginning of the nineteenth, reaches
back to the same political ideologies defended by the feudal lord
in his struggle against the bourgeoisie of his day. And precisely
because the Pure Theory of Law draws the ultimate conclusions
from the originally anti-ideological positivist philosophy and
legal theory of the nineteenth century, it stands in starkest
opposition to the epigones who renounce Kantian transcendental philosophy and legal positivism.

§ 12. The Law as Coercive Norm

The formal category of norm—the category designated by
'ought'—yields only the genus, not the *differentia specifica*, of the
law. Nineteenth-century legal theory agreed for the most part that
the legal norm is a coercive norm (a norm providing for coercion),
and that precisely thereby the legal norm is distinguished from
other norms. Here the Pure Theory of Law continues in the
tradition of nineteenth-century positivist legal theory. According to
the Pure Theory, the consequence attached in the reconstructed
legal norm to a certain condition is the coercive act of the state—
comprising punishment and the civil or administrative use of
coercion—whereby only the conditioning material fact is
qualified as an unlawful act, and only the conditioned material
fact is qualified as the consequence of the unlawful act. What
makes certain human behaviour illegal—a delict (in the broadest
sense of the word)—is neither some sort of immanent quality
nor some sort of connection to a metalegal norm, to a moral
value, a value transcending the positive law. Rather, what makes
certain behaviour a delict is simply and solely that this behaviour
is set in the reconstructed legal norm as the condition of a
specific consequence, it is simply and solely that the positive legal
system responds to this behaviour with a coercive act.

§ 13. The Concept of the Unlawful Act

From the standpoint of immanence, which the Pure Theory of
Law supplants, the concept of the unlawful act undergoes a
fundamental reinterpretation. What is dispositive for the concept

of the unlawful act is not the legislator's motive, not the circumstance that a material fact is undesirable to the norm-issuing authority, that it is, inexactly expressed, socially harmful (one should say only that it is so regarded by the legislator). Rather, what is dispositive is simply and solely the position that the material fact in question has in the reconstructed legal norm, namely, its position as the condition for the specific response of the law, for the coercive act (the action the state takes). An unlawful act is behaviour that is determined as condition in the reconstructed legal norm, behaviour of the human being who is subject to the coercive act that is established as consequence in the reconstructed legal norm. As behaviour of the human being addressed by the coercive act, the material fact of an unlawful act is distinguished from all other conditions of the consequence of the unlawful act. If (as in primitive legal systems or as in the case of an unlawful act imputed to a legal person [to a corporation, for example]) the consequence of an unlawful act is directed against someone other than the one responsible for the material fact of the unlawful act, this always presupposes that some sort of connection between the two of them is assumed by the legislator, whether that connection be real or fictitious. This is referred to as vicarious liability. Thus, the murderer's family is liable for his act, the prince is liable for delicts committed by his subjects, and the citizenry is liable for violations of law by state officials (collective liability). Between the real subject of the unlawful act and the object of the consequence of the unlawful act, there always exists a physical or legal identity.

By way of this line of reasoning, the unlawful act, an apparent negation of law from the standpoint of legal policy, becomes a specific condition of the law. And only thereby does the unlawful act become a possible object of legal cognition, for legal cognition can conceive of the unlawful act, too, only as law. The concept of the unlawful act gives up its extra-systemic position, where only a pre-scientific naïve jurisprudence can maintain it, and takes an intra-systemic position. Ethics and theology—both of them normative modes of cognition—function in exactly this way when, in the theodicy (in their attempt to interpret the world as a system of the good), they strip evil of its original character as a sheer negation of the good in order to account for evil only as a condition for realizing the good—with the idea that evil leads in the end to atonement and so to the victory of the good. The Pure Theory of Law unravels the notion that someone involved in the material fact of an unlawful act is 'breaking' or 'violating' the law. The Pure Theory shows that the law cannot be broken or violated by way of the unlawful act, any more than the law arrives at its essential function only by way of the unlawful act. The unlawful act does not represent an interruption in the existence of the law (as the traditional view would have one believe), but exactly the opposite: it is by way of the unlawful act that the existence of the law proves itself, for this existence consists in the validity of the law, that is, in the 'ought' of the coercive act as the consequence of the unlawful act.

On this point, too, the Pure Theory of Law runs counter to the legal theory of our time. The latter, strictly in keeping with its shift to natural law, would dispense with the coercive element as an empirical criterion of the law, holding that the law can be recognized by its intrinsic value, by its agreement with an idea of law.[24] Only if the binding force of the law is based on direct intuition of the value of the law—supposing positive law to be the offshoot of an absolute, that is, a divine or natural order— only then is the provision of coercion unnecessary to the law. For only then does the validity of the law, exactly like the validity of absolute morality, rest on the internal coercion that accompanies the intuitive conviction that the law is binding. This is a view clearly rooted in the natural law.

§ 14. The Law as Social Technique

(a) Efficacy of the Legal System

To view the law (considered purely positivistically) as simply an external coercive system, however, is to conceive of it merely as a specific social technique. What is socially desired is brought about or pursued by attaching a consequence to human behaviour that is the opposite of what is desired—the conse-

---

[24] On the 'idea of law', see § 10, n. 18, above, and Supplementary Note 4, in appendix I.

quence, namely, of a coercive act (the coercive deprivation of something good, such as life, liberty, or property). The legal system is obviously taking as its point of departure the assumption that the human beings whose behaviour it governs consider this coercive act an evil to be avoided. The purpose of the legal system is to induce human beings—by means of the notion of this evil threatening them if they behave in a certain way, opposite what is desired—to behave in the desired way. In this motivation lies the efficacy aimed at by the legal system. With an eye to efficacy, the content of legal norms (like that of social norms generally) is limited to human behaviour, for only the human being, endowed with reason and will, can be motivated by the notion of a norm, motivated to behave in conformity with that norm. So it is, too, that other material facts consisting in acts or forbearances of a human being, so-called incidents, appear as such in the content of legal norms only in essential connection with human behaviour, as its condition or consequence. When primitive legal systems direct the consequences of unlawful acts not only against human beings but also against animals and inanimate things, attempting thereby to govern the behaviour of non-human subjects too, it is because primitive animism holds that animals and things also have souls, that is, animism interprets non-human behaviour entirely by analogy to human behaviour.

(b) Secondary Norm

If, with an eye to the purpose of the legal system, one presupposes the requirement that human beings ought to behave so as to avoid the threatened coercive act, then one can break down the legal system into an aggregate of norms that appear to command the behaviour that the law aims to bring about. Examples would be such norms as, say, 'one ought not to steal', 'one ought to pay back a loan', and so on. Here one must keep in mind, however, that the connection to the coercive act, essential for the legal character of the norm, remains unexpressed. Thus, the norm that establishes sanction-avoiding behaviour—behaviour the legal system aims to bring about—is a legal norm only on the presupposition that it is saying something (in abbreviated form for the sake of convenience) that the reconstructed legal norm alone states fully and correctly: given, as condition, behaviour opposite that which the norm establishes as sanction-avoiding, then a coercive act is to be forthcoming as consequence. This reconstructed legal norm is the legal norm in its primary form.[25] The norm establishing sanction-avoiding behaviour can only be regarded, then, as a secondary legal norm. To be sure, the unlawful act (the condition of the coercive act) represents something like a negation, a kind of contradiction in relation to the material fact that the secondary norm establishes as obligatory, that is, in relation to sanction-avoiding behaviour, behaviour the legal system aims to bring about. But the material fact of an unlawful act is not a logical contradiction, not even in relation to the secondary norm establishing as obligatory the opposite material fact. Such a contradiction can exist only between two 'ought'-propositions or two 'is'-propositions, never between a proposition stating an 'ought' and one stating an 'is'—only between two norms, then, and not between a norm ('ought') and a material fact ('is'). A logical contradiction is represented by the figure, 'A ought to be, and not-A ought to be', but not by the figure, 'A ought to be, and not-A is'. 'Contrariety to norm'[26] is a completely different category from logical contradiction. While the opposition between a material fact and the norm establishing as obligatory the opposite material fact cannot be characterized as logical opposition, it can perhaps be characterized as teleological opposition, where *telos* is understood as objective purpose. The traditional concepts of illegality and legality—the concepts, that is, of behaviour contrary to the law and behaviour conforming to the law—are obviously geared to the secondary legal norm as the expression of legal purpose. One may make use of these traditional concepts with the qualification that what is meant by the former is behaviour conditioning the coercive act, and by the latter, behaviour avoiding the coercive act.

---

[25] 'legal norm in its primary form' ('*Rechtsnorm in ihrer primären Gestalt*'). See § 11(*b*), text at n. 21.

[26] 'Contrariety to norm' ('*Normwidrigkeit*'). Happily, most other members of the 'contrary-to' ('-*widrig*') family have familiar English-language equivalents, e.g. 'illegal' ('*rechtswidrig*') and 'unconstitutional' ('*verfassungswidrig*'). See also § 31(*h*), text at nn. 54–5.

(c) Motives for Obeying the Law

It is difficult to decide whether human behaviour that conforms to the legal system is actually an effect of the notion engendered by the threat of a coercive act. Certainly, in many cases, completely different motives lead to the state of affairs that the law aims to bring about. The motive is by no means always fear of sanction or of the coercive act being carried out; there are religious and moral reasons for doing this or that, there is regard for social custom, concern about social ostracism, and very often there is simply no stimulus to behave contrary to law—all of which bring reality into conformity with the law. As we shall see below,[27] this relation of correspondence between the legal system and the actual behaviour of human beings, a relation significant for the validity of the legal system,[28] is not necessarily traceable to the efficacy of the legal system. It may be traced instead to those ideologies in particular whose function it is to bring about or to support such correspondence.

The mode specific to the law, namely, the linking of a human being's behaviour, regarded as socially harmful, with a coercive act, perceived by that human being to be an evil, lends itself to the pursuit of any social purpose whatever. The law is characterized not as an end but as a specific means, a characterization that shows clearly why the secondary legal norm formulated above cannot be an essential expression of the law—not in itself, that is, without considering the reconstructed legal norm linking legal condition with legal consequence. The law is a coercive apparatus having in and of itself no political or ethical value, a coercive apparatus whose value depends, rather, on ends that transcend the law *qua* means. This interpretation, too, of the material fact to be comprehended as law is free of every ideology. This material fact is recognized unequivocally as historically conditioned, which in turn offers insight into the intrinsic connection between the social technique of a coercive system and a societal state of affairs to be maintained by way of that technique. What this state of affairs comes to—whether, as the socialists claim, it has in particular the character of exploitative class domination—is irrelevant from the standpoint

---

[27] At § 30(a).
[28] 'validity of the legal system' ('*Geltung der Rechtsordnung*').

of the Pure Theory of Law. The Pure Theory does not consider the ends pursued and achieved by the legal system, but considers only the legal system itself. And in considering the legal system without reference to its ends, and therefore not as a possible cause of a certain effect (the means-end relation being simply a special case of the causal connection), the Pure Theory considers the legal system *qua* normatively autonomous meaning.

§ 15. Denying the 'Ought'

Normative meaning, thus understood, is denied altogether from time to time. One views the law, that is, lawmaking acts, solely as a means of bringing about certain behaviour on the part of those human beings to whom the acts are directed; one views lawmaking acts, then, as causes of certain effects. And one believes that in the regularity of a certain pattern of human behaviour, one can comprehend the legal system. One thereby consciously ignores the normative meaning that accompanies lawmaking acts, for one believes that one cannot accept the meaning of an 'ought' that differs from 'is'. The assertion (of the legislator or the legal theorist) that whoever steals ought to be punished is regarded, then, as simply an attempt to induce human beings to forbear from theft because others punish thieves; it is regarded as an enterprise to engender in human beings certain notions whose motivating force induces them to behave in an appropriate way. The legal position, that one 'ought' not to steal or that one 'ought' to punish thieves, is broken down into determinations of fact—namely, that some people try to induce others to forbear from theft or to punish thieves, and that people, by and large, do forbear from theft and do punish thieves. One sees in the law (as in the connection between human beings who make the law and those who carry it out) an enterprise comparable, say, to that of a hunter who sets out bait to lure game into a trap. The comparison is apt not only because of the common connection to motivation, but also in so far as there is deception, considering the view described here, when the law is represented (by the legislator or by jurisprudence) as norm. From this viewpoint, no 'norms' are 'given' at all, and the assertion that this or that 'ought' to be the case has—

contrary to the assumption of the Pure Theory of Law—no meaning specific to the positive law, no meaning different in any way from that of morality. From this viewpoint, it is causally interconnected natural events alone that are considered, it is legal acts only in their facticity and not the specific meaning that accompanies these acts. This specific meaning—the norm or the 'ought' with which the law represents itself and is represented by jurisprudence—turns up as sheer 'ideology', and this is true even of meaning that has been refined by the Pure Theory of Law and freed of all absolute moral value. As 'reality'—and so, as the object of scientific cognition—there is only the physico-psychical event subject to the law of cause and effect, that is to say, there is only nature.

§ 16. The Normative Meaning of the Law

The question is left open here of whether social phenomena can be comprehended at all from such a viewpoint, whether it is not the case that, in a view like this, everything social must dissolve without remainder and disappear altogether as a particular object of cognition. For there is indeed much to be said on behalf of the claim that the social sphere is essentially ideological in character, that it is only as ideology in contrast with reality that society contrasts with nature at all. In any case, what is certain is that from this viewpoint, the specific meaning of the law is completely lost. If one deprives the norm or the 'ought' of meaning, then there will be no meaning in the assertions that something is legally allowed, something is legally proscribed, this belongs to me, that belongs to you, X has a right to do this, Y is obligated to do that, and so on. In short, all the thousands of statements in which the life of the law is manifest daily will have lost their significance. For it is one thing to say that A is legally obligated to turn over 1,000 talers to B, and quite another to say that there is a certain chance that A will in fact turn over 1,000 talers to B. And it is one thing to say that, in terms of a statute, certain behaviour is a delict and, in conformity with the statute, is to be punished, and quite another to say that whoever has behaved in this way will in all probability be punished. The immanent meaning when the legislator addresses the authority applying the statute, the meaning when this authority (in the judicial decision and the administrative act) addresses the citizen, and when this citizen (in the private law transaction) addresses another citizen—this immanent meaning is not comprehended with a statement on the probable course of future behaviour. Such a statement stems from a transcendent viewpoint. It does not answer the specifically legal question of what is lawful, but answers instead the metalegal question of what is happening now and what will presumably happen in the future. If the normative meaning of the law is simply an 'ideology', then a theory of law that aims to comprehend the immanent meaning of the law—the law as it represents itself to the organs that make and apply the law and to the law-seeking public—focuses on what is unique to an ideology.

The Pure Theory of Law, in particular, reflects full awareness of this. Indeed, in stripping the positive law 'ought' of its character as a metaphysico-absolute value (leaving the 'ought' simply as the expression of the linking, in the reconstructed legal norm, of condition and consequence), the Pure Theory itself has cleared the way to the very viewpoint that yields insight into the ideological character of the law. The Pure Theory of Law is well aware that the specifically normative meaning of certain material facts, the meaning characterized as 'law', is the result not of a necessary interpretation but of a possible interpretation, possible only given a certain basic presupposition, which will be spelled out below.[29] And the Pure Theory is well aware that one cannot prove the existence of the law as one proves the existence of natural material facts and the natural laws governing them, that one cannot adduce compelling arguments to refute a posture like theoretical anarchism, which refuses to see anything but naked power where jurists speak of the law. However, the Pure Theory of Law does not consider it necessary to dispense therefore with the category designated by 'ought' altogether, and so to dispense with a normative theory of law—that is, the epistemological exploration and systematic treatment of the intellectual substance borne by natural acts and first giving them legal meaning. The possibility and the necessity of a normative theory of law is shown by the very existence of legal science over a millennium,

[29] See §§ 27–9.

which, in the guise of dogmatic jurisprudence, serves—so long as there is law at all—the intellectual requirements of those who concern themselves with the law. There is no reason to leave these thoroughly legitimate requirements unsatisfied and to dispense with such legal science. To replace it with legal sociology is impossible, for legal sociology focuses on an entirely different problem. So long as there is religion, there must be dogmatic theology, not to be replaced by the psychology or sociology of religion; and, similarly, so long as there is law, there will be normative legal theory. Its rank in the overall scheme of the cognitive sciences is a secondary question. What is called for is not the abandonment of this legal science along with the category of norm, the category designated by 'ought', but the restriction of legal science to its object of cognition and the critical clarification of its methods.

§ 17. 'Ought' and 'Is' of the Law

That one can accept the law (compared with natural reality) as ideology and nevertheless demand a pure theory of the law— that is, a theory free of ideology—is by no means as contradictory as it appears to be. The term 'ideology' is ambiguous, to be sure, marking on one occasion the assertion of the ideal in opposition to the natural, while representing on another occasion a notion that veils reality by transfiguring or distorting it. Quite apart from that ambiguity, however, it should also be noted that different ideologies overlap occasionally, that several strata are often distinguishable within the ideological sphere, and that, therefore, the opposition between ideology and reality becomes relative. If one considers the positive law *qua* normative system in its relation to the reality of actual events that the positive law claims ought to conform to it (even if the events by no means always do conform), then one can qualify the positive law as 'ideology'. If one considers the positive law *qua* normative system in its relation to a 'higher' system that claims the positive law ought to conform to it, say, natural law or some imagined absolute value of justice, then the positive law represents the 'real' existing law, and natural law or justice represents ideology. The Pure Theory of Law preserves its anti-ideological stance by seeking to isolate representations of the positive law from every natural law ideology of justice. It does not discuss the possibility of the validity of a system higher than the positive law. The Pure Theory of Law confines itself to the positive law, thereby preventing legal science from either passing off the positive law as a higher system or justifying the positive law on the basis of a higher system. And the Pure Theory of Law prevents misuse of the discrepancy between some presupposed absolute value of justice and the positive law, prevents its misuse as a legal argument against the validity of the positive law. The Pure Theory of Law is the theory of legal positivism.

IV

Overcoming the Dualism of Legal Theory

§ 18. Natural Law Origins of the Dualism of Objective Law and Subjective Right

General legal theory, as developed by nineteenth-century positivist jurisprudence, is marked by a dualism that dominates legal theory as a whole, rending all its problems.[30] This dualism is a remnant of natural law theory, the theory supplanted by general legal theory. The dualism of natural law theory has been shown[31] to consist in the assumption that, above the state system of positive law, there is a legal system that is superior, divine, based on reason or natural law. And—a point that cannot be over-emphasized—the function of this higher system, at least according to the classical representatives of seventeenth- and eighteenth-century natural law theory, was essentially that of conservative legitimization. Nineteenth-century positivism, as already indicated,[32] does not dispense entirely with an appeal to a supra-positive value as a legitimization of the law; but its efforts along these lines are only indirect, made beneath the surface of its concepts, so to speak. Today, positive law is justified less by appeal to a higher law, different from positive law, than by appeal to the concept of law itself. It is not this immanent, obscure dualism that is under discussion here, but the manifestly trans-systemic dualism that turns up in the distinction between objective law and subjective right, between private and public law, and in many other antithetical pairings, not least of all in the antagonism between law and state. And the function of

---

[30] Kelsen's more explicit formulation is that dualism rends the problems of legal theory by 'doubling the object of cognition'; see esp. §48(e), text at n. 71.
[31] See § 8.
[32] See §§ 10–11(a).

this dualism, appearing in multifarious forms and taking divergent twists and turns, is not simply to legitimize the positive legal system, but also to set certain constraints on the shaping of its content. If legitimization of the legal system applies especially to the opposition between law and state, the setting of constraints on the content of the legal system applies unmistakably to the distinction between objective law and subjective right. The opposition between private and public law, on the other hand, is extraordinarily ambiguous, and therefore the determination of its ideological function is not uniform either.

§ 19. The Concept of Subjective Right

When general legal theory claims that its object of enquiry, the law, is given not only in an objective sense but also in a subjective sense,[33] it builds into its very foundation a basic contradiction, that is, the dualism of objective law and subjective right. For general legal theory is thereby claiming that law—as objective law—is norm, a complex of norms, a system, and claiming at the same time that law—as subjective right—is interest or will, something altogether different from objective law and therefore impossible to subsume under any general concept common to both. This contradiction cannot be removed even by claiming a connection between objective law and subjective right, by claiming that the latter is defined as interest that is protected by the former, as will that is recognized or guaranteed by the former. In line with its original function, the dualism of objective law and subjective right expresses the idea that the latter precedes the former logically as well as temporally. The notion is decisive: subjective rights—above all, property rights, which are, by way of original acquisition, the prototype of the subjective right—arise prior to, and independently of, the objective law, which emerges only later as a state system protecting, recognizing, and guaranteeing subjective rights. This view is most evident among representatives of the Historical

[33] 'law . . . in an objective sense . . . also in a subjective sense' ('Recht . . . in einem objektiven . . . auch in einem subjektiven Sinn'). The distinction underlies the opposition between 'objective law' ('objektives Recht') or legal system, and 'subjective right' ('subjektives Recht').

School,[34] who not only inaugurated nineteenth-century legal positivism, but also essentially determined the conceptual framework of general legal theory. For example, one reads in Dernburg's treatise:

> Historically speaking, rights in the subjective sense existed for a very long time before a conscious political order developed. They were based on the personality of individuals, and on the respect these individuals were able first to win for themselves and their property, and then to enforce. It was only by way of abstraction that contemplation of existing subjective rights gradually led to the concept of the legal system. It is therefore unhistorical and incorrect to view rights in the subjective sense as nothing but emanations of law in the objective sense.[35]

§ 20. The Concept of Legal Subject or Person

Closely related to the concept of subjective right—indeed, at bottom simply a variation on the same theme—is the concept of legal subject or 'person'[36] *qua* bearer of the subjective right, a concept essentially modelled on the property owner. Here, too, the notion of a legal entity independent of the legal system is decisive. It is the notion of a legal subjectivity that finds, so to speak, the existing subjective right in the individual or in certain collectives, a legal subjectivity that has only to recognize the subjective right—and, indeed, must necessarily recognize it lest the subjective right lose its character as 'law'. The opposition between law (in the objective sense) and legal subjectivity, a logical contradiction within the theory if the theory claims that

[34] The German Historical School is most closely associated with Friedrich Carl von Savigny, who defended a 'strict historical method' that aims 'to trace every established system [of law] to its root, and thus discover an organic principle, whereby that which still has life, may be separated from that which is lifeless and only belongs to history'. Savigny, *Of the Vocation of Our Age for Legislation and Jurisprudence*, trans. Abraham Hayward (London: Littlewood, 1831), 137.

[35] Heinrich Dernburg, *System des Römischen Rechts*, 8th edn., pt. i (Berlin: H. W. Müller, 1911), 65.

[36] ' "person" ' (' "*Person*" '). We have followed Kelsen's practice—here, and occasionally elsewhere—of placing 'person' within quotation marks when it is used, without attributive modifiers, as shorthand (in the tradition) for the legal subject. In the Pure Theory, by contrast, 'person' is a personifying expression for the unity of a complex of norms, a legal system. See § 25(a)–(f).

both exist at the same time, is expressed most strikingly in the following: the meaning of the objective law as a heteronomous norm is the bond, is in fact coercion, while the essence of legal personality is declared to be precisely the negation of every bond, namely, liberty in terms of self-determination or autonomy. Puchta writes:

The basic concept of the law is liberty . . . [and] the abstract concept of liberty is: the possibility of self-determination. . . . The human being is the subject of the law because this possibility of self-determination is attributed to him, because, that is to say, he has a will.[37]

§ 21. Ideological Significance of the Concepts 'Subjective Right' and 'Legal Subject'

The fiction in this characterization of the concept of legal personality is obvious. For if one can speak of an individual's self-determination in the legal sphere at all, it is in the field of so-called private law, with reference to the law-creating material fact of the contract; but even there, autonomy exists only in a very restricted, figurative sense. One cannot grant rights to oneself, because one's right presupposes another's obligation, and a legal connection such as this can only be made—in conformity with the objective legal system—by way of a consonant expression of will on the part of two individuals. And even this forges a legal connection only in so far as the contract is established by the objective law as a law-creating material fact. So it is that the characterization 'legal' stems in the end from precisely this objective law, and not from the legal subject of the objective law; even in private law, then, there is no complete autonomy.

The ideological function is easy to see in this utterly self-contradictory characterization of the concepts of subjective right and legal subject. The notion to be maintained is that the subjective right, which really means private property, is a category transcending the objective law, it is an institution putting unavoidable constraints on the shaping of the content of

---

[37] Georg Friedrich Puchta, *Cursus der Institutionen*, 10th edn., vol. i (Leipzig: Breitkopf & Härtel, 1893), 4, 5, 6.

the legal system. The concept of a subjective right that is different from, and independent of, the objective law becomes all the more important if the objective law—that is, the legal system still guaranteeing the institution of private property—is recognized as a changeable and, indeed, constantly changing system, created by way of human discretion and not based on the eternal will of the Deity or on reason or nature. And such a concept of subjective right becomes still more important if the legal system is created democratically. The thought of a right that is different from, and independent of, the objective law, a right that is no less and, indeed, perhaps even more 'law' than the objective law—this thought should protect the institution of private property from suppression by the legal system. Since property has always been a part of individual liberty, of autonomous personality, it is not difficult to understand why the ideology of the subjective right attaches to the ethical value of liberty thus understood. A system that does not recognize the human being as a free personality in this sense, a system that does not guarantee subjective rights, should not be considered a legal system at all.

§ 22. The Concept of Legal Relation

It is entirely in keeping with this ideology of the subjective right that the relation between law and society, especially that between law and the economic order, is viewed as a relation between form and content, and that legal relations are interpreted as connections existing within the social milieu, 'human relations' determined only outwardly by the law. (There is, in particular, a branch of traditional jurisprudence that passes itself off as 'sociological' while in fact simply pursuing natural law tendencies.) And it is in keeping with the dualism of objective law and subjective right that legal relations are distinguished as material or personal, depending on whether the connection in question is, respectively, between legal subject and legal object— person and thing—or between subjects. The material legal relation—the material legal connection *par excellence*—is property, and the very distinction between material and personal legal relations is modelled on it. Property is defined as a person's exclusive control over a thing, and it is thereby distinguished fundamentally from those claim rights that establish strictly personal legal relations. This distinction, important in the systematization of the civil law, is also clearly ideological in character. The objection repeatedly raised against it is that a person's legal control over a thing simply amounts to a certain legal relation of the subject to other subjects—namely, in their obligation not to interfere with the property owner's possibility of disposition of a thing, in other words, the legal possibility that one party may exclude all other parties from enjoyment of the thing. If the distinction of the material legal relation is maintained in spite of this objection, it is clearly because a definition of property as a relation between person and thing disguises the socio-economically decisive function of property, a function characterized in socialist theory (never mind whether correctly or incorrectly) as 'exploitation'. In any case, it is a function that consists precisely in the connection of the property owner to all other subjects, who are excluded from access to his things, and who are obligated by the objective law to respect his exclusive power of disposition. But precisely this point is resolutely rejected by traditional legal theory when it denies that the subjective right—the legal right of one subject—is merely the reflex of the legal obligation of another subject. Again and again, and with the greatest vigour, its representatives emphasize the primary character of the legal right. Indeed, they identify the legal right straightaway with the law—with, that is to say, law in the subjective sense.

§ 23. The Concept of Legal Obligation

The other form of law in the subjective sense, legal obligation, is treated with conspicuous disinterest by general legal theory. Occasionally the claim is even made that obligation is not a legal concept at all, that there are no legal obligations, only moral obligations, and that there are, in the law, only subjective rights. The essential function of a system, however, especially of a coercive system like that of the law, can only be to bind normatively those individuals subject to the system; and this normative bond can only be characterized by the word 'obligation'. Even moral obligation expresses nothing other than the binding of the individual by means of the validity of a moral order or system. However, given the role played by the concept of subjective right *qua* category of private property, to extend that concept to legal obligation does in fact make little sense. Indeed, everything that 'subjective right' is able to accomplish in terms of ideological theory will be called directly into question if 'subjective right' is confronted, in the concept of legal obligation, with an equal, not to mention a primary, element.

§ 24. Reducing Law in the Subjective Sense to Objective Law

(a) Legal Norm as Legal Obligation

At exactly this point, the Pure Theory of Law launches its critique of the received academic opinion by bringing the concept of legal obligation emphatically to the fore. Here, too, the Pure Theory is simply drawing the obvious conclusion from certain basic ideas already expressed in nineteenth-century positivist theory but not developed beyond their relatively modest beginnings. The Pure Theory recognizes in legal obligation simply the individualized legal norm, that is, a legal norm (establishing [as obligatory] certain behaviour) in its connection to the concrete behaviour of a particular individual. And the Pure Theory completely emancipates the concept of legal obligation from that of moral obligation by interpreting the former as follows: a human being is legally obligated to behave in a certain way in so far as the opposite behaviour is set in the legal norm as the condition for a coercive act qualified as the consequence of an unlawful act. If the coercive act is directed against someone other than the human being whose behaviour is the condition for the consequence, and whose behaviour is therefore (in this sense) the content of the obligation, then one can speak of liability; thus, one can differentiate the concepts of obligation and liability, whereby liability emerges as a particular type of obligation. Legal obligation, then, is recognized as the sole essential function of the objective law. Every reconstructed legal norm must necessarily establish a legal obligation; it may establish a legal right as well.

(b) Legal Norm as Legal Right

A legal right exists where an expression of will is included among the conditions for the consequence of an unlawful act, an expression of will that addresses this consequence and that is to be brought in the form of a complaint or claim by the party whose interests were violated by the unlawful act. Only in its connection to the violated party is the legal norm individualized as a legal right; in making itself available to a subject for the assertion of his interests, the legal norm becomes the right of that subject, that is, a subjective right—law in a subjective sense different from legal obligation. As legal right, law in the subjective sense is not independent of the objective law, for there is such a thing as a subjective right only because and in so far as the objective law normatively regulates it. The legal right is quite simply one possible way of shaping the content of the objective law; it is by no means a necessary way. It is one particular technique that the law can, but need not, use—the technique specific to the capitalistic legal system as a system based on the institution of private property and so taking special account of individual interests. This technique, moreover, does not even dominate all parts of the capitalistic legal system, turning up fully developed only in so-called private law and in certain parts of administrative law. Even modern criminal law goes beyond it, when the state's attorney (instead of the violated party), acting as 'complainant' by virtue of his office, sets into motion the process wherein the consequence of the unlawful act is to be realized.

With this insight into the essence of what is called law in the subjective sense, the Pure Theory of Law eliminates the dualism of objective law and subjective right. The subjective right is not different from objective law; it is itself objective law. For there is a subjective right (*qua* legal right) only in so far as the objective law is at the disposal of a concrete subject. Similarly, the legal obligation (the other form of law in the subjective sense) is itself objective law, for there is a legal obligation only in so far as the objective law aims—with the consequence it establishes for an unlawful act—at a concrete subject. If the subjective right is reduced in this way to objective law, if it is brought within the objective law, then every ideological misuse of it is precluded. Above all, the concept of law is no longer restricted to one particular technique giving shape to the legal system. Even the historically conditioned formation of law in a capitalistic system is accounted for within the concept of law.

(c) Legal Right as Participation in Creating Law

The essence of the subjective right—*qua* legal right, characteristic of private law—may be recognized in the fact that the interested party's complaint or claim, his expression of will addressing the consequence of an unlawful act, is included as an essential component in the process whereby the individual norm of the judicial decision is created, a decision attaching the concrete consequence of an unlawful act to the concrete material fact of an unlawful act. If this is recognized as the essence of the subjective right *qua* legal right, then acknowledging a subjective right amounts to granting participation in creating law.

From this standpoint, one can understand other material facts as well, characterized as 'subjective rights' but, unlike the private law right, not exercised in an expression of will addressing the consequence of an unlawful act. There are, in particular, so-called 'political' rights. One is accustomed to characterizing a political right as the power to influence the formation of the will of the state, that is, the power to participate directly or indirectly in creating the legal system within which the 'will of the state' is expressed. But what one has in mind here (when, as is usually the case, reference is to the legal system personified as the 'will of the state') is simply the general phenomenal form of the legal norms making up the legal system—that is to say, statutes. The essential characteristic of the democratic form of state is that people subject to the statutes participate in legislation, in contradistinction to the autocratic form of state, which excludes its subjects from any participation in forming the will of the state. Legislation in a democracy comes about in two ways. Either it is carried out directly by 'the people', that is, by those subject to the statutes—which circumstance (in the so-called direct democracy) corresponds to the subjective right of each citizen to participate in the legislative assembly of the people, to join in speaking and taking decisions there. Or, alternatively, legislation is owing only indirectly to the people; that is to say, legislation is carried out by a parliament elected by the people.

Here the process of forming the will of the state (general law creation) divides into two phases: election of the parliament, and then enactment of statutes by the elected members of parliament. Corresponding to this alternative, there is the subjective right of a greater or smaller circle of electors, namely, the so-called right of suffrage, and there is the subjective right of the relatively few who are elected, namely, the right to membership in the parliament, the right to join in speaking and voting there. All these are political rights. If they are characterized by the fact that they grant to the right-holder a role in forming the will of the state, then even the subjective right of the private law is a political right, for here, too, the right-holder participates in forming the will of the state. The will of the state is expressed no less in the individual norm of the judicial decision than in the general norm of the statute. And if both the subjective right of the private law and the political right can be subsumed under one and the same concept of legal right, it is simply because the same legal function—the law-creating function—is expressed in both; that is to say, in both cases, those subject to the law participate in creating the law. The so-called 'political' right in the narrower sense of the word guarantees participation in creating the general norm, and the private law right guarantees participation in creating the individual norm.

If one considers the subjective right (*qua* legal right) as a particular shaping of the law-creating function, then the opposition between objective law and subjective right disappears completely. And then the primary character of the legal obligation shows up especially clearly against the secondary character of the legal right. While the obligation appears as the intrinsic function of every legal norm without exception, the right appears either (*qua* private law right) simply as an institution of a capitalistic legal system, or (*qua* 'political' right) simply as a fixture of a democratic legal system.

§ 25. Analysing the Concept of Person

The way is thus cleared for recognizing the concept of legal subject or person as simply an artificial aid to thought, a heuristic concept created by legal cognition—under the pressure of a personifying, anthropomorphic legal language—in order to illustrate the data to be dealt with. 'Person' is simply a personifying expression for the unity of a bundle of legal obligations and legal rights, that is, the unity of a complex of norms. And this insight protects against misleading hypostatizations that [in failing to distinguish between the legal and the biologico-psychological concepts of person] have the effect of doubling the law *qua* object of cognition.

(a) 'Physical' Person[38]

Now at last the old challenge of positivist legal theory can be met completely—the challenge, namely, of comprehending 'physical' and legal person as essentially alike. 'Physical person' is not, as traditional theory claims, the human being. That is a biologico-psychological concept, not a legal one. It expresses no entity proper to the law or to legal cognition, for the law does not comprehend the human being in his totality, with all his mental and physical functions. Rather, the law establishes only particular human acts as obligations or rights. In other words, the human being belongs to the community constituted by a legal system not in his entirety, but only in certain of his acts and forbearances, namely, those that are governed by the norms of the community's legal system. Only thus is it possible for one human being to belong to several divergent legal communities at the same time, and possible for his behaviour to be governed by different legal systems. To say that the concept of human being used in the natural sciences must be distinguished from the legal concept of person is not to say that the 'person' is a particular type of human being; rather, it is to say that these represent two completely different entities. The legal concept of person or legal subject expresses simply the unity of a plurality of obligations and rights, which is really the unity of a plurality of norms establishing these obligations and rights. The 'physical' person corresponding to the individual human being is the personification

---

[38] ' "Physical" Person' (' *"physische" Person*'). In the Pure Theory, as Kelsen explains below, 'physical person' does not mean the human being. As a way of flagging this idiosyncratic use, Kelsen—here, and occasionally elsewhere—places 'physical' within quotation marks, a practice we have extended throughout these subsections.

—the personified expression—of the unity of norms governing the behaviour of one human being; the 'physical' person is the 'bearer' of all these obligations and rights. That is to say— stripping the notion of its misleading biologico-psychological character (misleading because it doubles the object of cognition)—the 'physical' person is the common point of imputation for the material facts of human behaviour that are normatively regulated as obligations and rights. The 'physical' person is the focal point, so to speak, of that subsystem whose norms establish these obligations and rights, and whose individualization emerges by way of connection to the behaviour of one and the same human being. While the individual human being is a natural reality, the 'physical' person is a heuristic notion of legal cognition—a notion that might well be dispensed with, that facilitates the exposition of the law, but is not necessary to it. This exposition must always go back ultimately to the norms governing human behaviour *qua* obligations and rights. That the human being is a legal personality, or has legal personality, means in the end simply that certain of his acts and forbearances are in one way or another the content of legal norms. Considering the distinction—strictly to be maintained—between human being and person, it is incorrect to say that the law imposes obligations on, and grants rights to, persons. Rather, the law imposes obligations on, and grants rights to, human beings. It is human behaviour that is the content of legal norms and therefore of obligations and rights, and human behaviour can only be the behaviour of individual human beings.

(b) 'Legal' Person

The so-called legal person, like the 'physical' person, is simply an expression of the unity of a complex of norms, the unity, that is, of a legal system governing the behaviour of a plurality of human beings. Either the legal person is the personification of a subsystem, which constitutes a subcommunity—the personification, say, of an association's charter, which constitutes the legal person of the association; or it is the personification of a comprehensive legal system, which constitutes a legal community encompassing all subcommunities, and which is customarily represented in the person of the state. The legal person,

again like the 'physical' person, has no natural, real existence.
What is 'real' in this natural sense is simply the human behaviour
that is governed by norms, which lend themselves to classification according to different points of view. The assumption that
the legal person is a reality different from individual human
beings, a reality, yet curiously imperceptible to the senses, or a
supra-individual social organism made up of individual human
beings—this is the naïve hypostatization of a thought, of a
heuristic legal notion. Just as the 'physical' person is hardly the
human being, so the legal person is hardly a supra-human being.
The obligations and rights of a legal person must be broken
down into obligations and rights of human beings, that is, into
norms governing human behaviour, establishing certain human
acts as obligations and rights. That the state legal system imposes
obligations on, or grants rights to, a legal person means that the
system turns the behaviour of a human being into obligation or
right without itself determining the individual subject of the
obligation or right. Such determination—by virtue of being
delegated by the state legal system—is left to the legal subsystem
whose unity is expressed in the legal person. Thus, obligations
are imposed on, and rights are granted to, individual human
beings indirectly, that is, mediated by the legal subsystem.

(c) Indirectly or Directly Imposing Obligations on, and Granting Rights to, Individual Human Beings

This division of functions between a comprehensive legal system
and its subsystems is possible because two elements can be
distinguished in the human behaviour that is the content of the
legal norm, and thus of the obligation and right. There is both a
personal (subjective) element and a material (objective) element,
namely, the subject of the act or forbearance, and the act or
forbearance itself—*who* does or forbears from doing, and *what*
is done or forborne. The complete norm determines both
elements. But a norm—and thus the accompanying obligation or
right—may well contain only one of these elements. Then it is
incomplete, and requires completion by way of another norm,
which determines the missing element. Norms that impose
obligations on, and grant rights to, a legal person to behave in a
certain way—as one usually puts it—are norms that determine

directly only the objective element, that is, only an act or a forbearance. They delegate to another norm the task of determining the subjective element, the individual responsible for the regulated behaviour. To say that a legal person has obligations and rights is not to deny that individual human beings have these obligations and rights; rather, it is simply to say that these obligations are imposed on, and these rights are granted to, individual human beings indirectly.

(d) Central Imputation

The obligations and rights of a legal person, because they refer to human behaviour, are always simply the obligations and rights of individual human beings. These human beings 'have' these obligations and rights not in the usual way—that is, individually—but collectively. That which one calls the property or assets of a legal person [of a corporation, for example] are the assets of those human beings making up the legal person. They are able to exercise control over these assets, however, not as they do over their individual assets, but only according to the provisions of the legal subsystem whose unity is represented in the legal person. If the legal person has a claim right, this amounts to a collective claim right of the members. The collective character of the right expresses itself, *inter alia*, in the fact that the exercise of the right proceeds not by way of every individual member, but by way of an organ designated by the subsystem. This human being is an organ of the legal community only because and in so far as his act, by virtue of being established by the legal subsystem constituting the legal community, can be connected to the unity of this system. This connection of a material fact to the unity of the system is also characterized as 'imputation', and the 'person' is accordingly a point of imputation. All acts of the legal person are acts of human beings, human acts that are imputed to the fictitious subject that one imagines the unity of a legal subsystem or comprehensive legal system to be. This central imputation, however, is an entirely different operation from the peripheral imputation mentioned earlier,[39] where a material fact is con-

[39] See § 11(b). On the distinction between central and peripheral imputation generally, see Supplementary Note 6, in appendix I.

nected not to the unity of the system but to another material fact within the system, that is, where two material facts are linked together in the reconstructed legal norm.

(e) Limitation of Liability

If the legal person has exercised its claim right—that is, if the human being acting as organ of the legal person has exercised the collective claim right of the human beings making up the community personified in the legal person—then the value of the assets acquired through execution of a settlement falls within the collective assets of the human beings making up this subcommunity. By the same token, if the legal person is obligated to perform a certain act, then, in the event of non-performance, the execution of a settlement is levied not against the individual assets of the members, but against their collective assets—still, of course, their assets. Limiting the execution of a settlement to the collective assets of the individuals making up the community that functions as a legal person—this so-called limitation of liability—is especially characteristic of legal persons in private law. It does not come into consideration—at any rate, not first and foremost—for legal persons in public law, especially not for the legal person of the state. As the personification of a comprehensive legal system, the legal person of the state encompasses all legal subsystems, and thus all 'physical' and legal persons incorporated in those subsystems; the legal person of the state is, therefore, the endpoint of central imputation.

(f) Ideological Significance of the Antinomy between Individual and Community

'Person' is understood as the personification of a norm complex and thus of a (more or less arbitrarily individualized) part of the system of objective law, a system comprising all the obligations and rights that it establishes, the obligations and rights of all 'persons', and creating among them an organic, that is, a systematic unity—so that the right of one is always the obligation of another, and right and obligation can never be isolated from each other. If 'person' is understood in this way, even the pseudo-antinomy between individual and community is dissolved, an antinomy under which traditional social philo-sophy is labouring when it asserts the individual *qua* whole and, at the same time, *qua* part of the community. From the standpoint of the objective system or that of the community constituted by it, there is no independent individual at all; that is, no independent individual can be comprehended as such by cognition focused on the social system. Only certain acts of the individual come under consideration, namely, those acts that form the content of the system, that are governed by the system. One can also express this by saying that the individual, considered in this way, exists only as a dependent component of the community. The individual *qua* independent whole bespeaks the same ideology of liberty that the specifically legal category of person [in the tradition] does.[40] And both have the function of erecting a bulwark against overstated claims of the social system constituting the community, claims that cannot be reconciled with certain interests. The individual in an apparently insoluble conflict with the community—this is simply an ideology in the struggle of certain interests to resist containment by a collective system.

§ 26. The Universalistic Character of the Pure Theory of Law

If the concept of subjective right, like the concept of legal subject, is stripped of every ideological function, if the veil of personifica-tion is lifted from actual legal connections, then what always emerge are, quite simply, legal connections between human beings, more precisely, between material facts of human behaviour, which are linked together by—that is, as the content of—the legal norm. The legal relation is the connection of two material facts, one of which consists in human behaviour established as legal obligation, the other, in human behaviour established as legal right. The Pure Theory of Law gives the lie to the notion that what is called law in the subjective sense—in all its manifestations, as legal right, legal obligation, legal subject— is different in kind from the objective law. In understanding so-called law in the subjective sense simply as a particular shaping

[40] On the ideological function, in the tradition, of the concepts of subjective right and legal subject or person, see e.g. the latter paragraph of § 21.

or a personification of the objective law, the Pure Theory renders ineffectual a subjectivistic attitude toward the law, the attitude served by the concept of so-called law in the subjective sense. It is the advocate's view, which considers the law only from the standpoint of the individual's interest, only in terms of what the law means for the individual, to what extent it is of use to him by serving his interests, or to what extent it is detrimental to him by threatening him with something untoward. This subjectivistic attitude toward the law is the characteristic posture of Roman jurisprudence, a posture that has emerged largely from the expert practice of lawyers representing individuals with just such interests at stake, a posture that was part of the reception of the Roman law generally. The posture of the Pure Theory of Law, on the other hand, is thoroughly objectivistic and universalistic. It looks, in principle, to the whole of the law, and seeks to comprehend each and every phenomenon only in systematic connection with all other phenomena, to comprehend in every legal component the function of the legal whole. In this sense, the Pure Theory of Law is a truly organic conception of the law. In conceiving of the law as organic, it does not understand thereby some supra-individual, supra-empirical—or metaphysical—entity of a biological or psychological sort, a notion concealing for the most part ethico-political postulates. Rather, the Pure Theory understands thereby simply and solely that the law is a system, and that therefore all legal problems are confronted and to be solved as systemic problems. Legal theory thus becomes as exact a structural analysis of the positive law as possible, an analysis free of all ethico-political value-judgments.

V

The Legal System and its Hierarchical Structure

§ 27. System as System of Norms

The law *qua* system—the legal system—is a system of legal norms. The first questions to answer here have been put by the Pure Theory of Law in the following way: what accounts for the unity of a plurality of legal norms, and why does a certain legal norm belong to a certain legal system?

A plurality of norms forms a unity, a system, an order, if the validity of the norms can be traced back to a single norm as the ultimate basis of validity. This basic norm *qua* common source constitutes the unity in the plurality of all norms forming a system. That a norm belongs to a certain system follows simply from the fact that the validity of the norm can be traced back to the basic norm constituting this system. Systems of norms can be distinguished into two different types according to type of basic norm, which really means, according to the nature of the highest principle of validity in the system. Norms of the first type are 'valid' by virtue of their substance; that is, the human behaviour specified by these norms is to be regarded as obligatory because the content of the norms has a directly evident quality that confers validity on it. And the content of these norms is qualified in this way because the norms can be traced back to a basic norm under whose content the content of the norms forming the system is subsumed, as the particular under the general. Norms of this type are the norms of morality. For example, the norms 'you shall not lie', 'you shall not cheat', 'keep your promise', and so on are derived from a basic norm of truthfulness. From the basic norm 'love your neighbour', one can derive the norms 'you shall not harm others', 'you shall help those in need', and so on.

The basic norm of a given moral order is of no further concern here. What matters is knowing that the many norms of a moral order are already contained in its basic norm, just as the particular is contained in the general; thus, all particular moral norms can be derived from the general basic norm by way of an act of intellect, namely, by way of a deduction from the general to the particular. The basic norm of morality has a substantive, static character.

§ 28. The Legal System as Chain of Creation

Norms of the second type of system, norms of the law, are not valid by virtue of their content. Any content whatever can be law; there is no human behaviour that would be excluded simply by virtue of its substance from becoming the content of a legal norm. The validity of a legal norm cannot be called into question on the ground that its content fails to correspond to some presupposed substantive value, say, a moral value. A norm is valid *qua* legal norm only because it was arrived at in a certain way—created according to a certain rule, issued or set according to a specific method. The law is valid only as positive law, that is, only as law that has been issued or set. In this necessary requirement of being issued or set, and in what it assures, namely, that the validity of the law will be independent of morality and comparable systems of norms—therein lies the positivity of the law. And therein lies the essential difference between the positive law and so-called natural law. For the norms of natural law, like those of morality, are deduced from a basic norm that by virtue of its content—as emanation of divine will, of nature, or of pure reason—is held to be directly evident. The basic norm of a positive legal system, however, is simply the basic rule according to which the norms of the legal system are created; it is simply the setting into place of the basic material fact of law creation. This basic norm, the point of departure for a process, has a thoroughly formal, dynamic character. Particular norms of the legal system cannot be logically deduced from this basic norm. Rather, they must be created by way of a special act issuing or setting them, an act not of intellect but of will. There are manifold forms for issuing or setting legal norms—custom or legislation in the case of general norms, adjudicative acts and private law transactions in the case of individual norms. Law creation by way of custom contrasts with all other forms of law creation, which, unlike custom, yield enacted law [*jus scriptum*]; custom is therefore a special case [*jus non scriptum*] of the making of law.

Tracing the various norms of a legal system back to a basic norm is a matter of showing that a particular norm was created in accordance with the basic norm. For example, one may ask why a certain coercive act is a legal act and thus belongs to a certain legal system—the coercive act of incarceration, say, whereby one human being deprives another of liberty. The answer is that this act was prescribed by a certain individual norm, a judicial decision. Suppose one asks further why this individual norm is valid, indeed, why it is valid as a component of a certain legal system. The answer is that this individual norm was issued in accordance with the criminal code. And if one asks about the basis of the validity of the criminal code, one arrives at the state constitution, according to whose provisions the criminal code was enacted by the competent authorities in a constitutionally prescribed procedure.

If one goes on to ask about the basis of the validity of the constitution, on which rest all statutes and the legal acts stemming from those statutes, one may come across an earlier constitution, and finally the first constitution, historically speaking, established by a single usurper or a council, however assembled. What is to be valid as norm is whatever the framers of the first constitution have expressed as their will—this is the basic presupposition of all cognition of the legal system resting on this constitution. Coercion is to be applied under certain conditions and in a certain way, namely, as determined by the framers of the first constitution or by the authorities to whom they have delegated appropriate powers—this is the schematic formulation of the basic norm of a legal system (a single-state legal system, which is our sole concern here).[41]

---

[41] See § 30(c) and, for greater detail, § 49(a), where Kelsen takes up the basic norm with reference to international law.

§ 29. Significance of the Basic Norm

The Pure Theory of Law works with this basic norm as a
hypothetical foundation. Given the presupposition that the basic
norm is valid, the legal system resting on it is also valid. The
basic norm confers on the act of the first legislator—and thus on
all other acts of the legal system resting on this first act—the
sense of 'ought', that specific sense in which legal condition is
linked with legal consequence in the reconstructed legal norm,
the paradigmatic form in which it must be possible to represent
all the data of the positive law.[42] Rooted in the basic norm,
ultimately, is the normative import of all the material facts
constituting the legal system. The empirical data given to legal
interpretation can be interpreted as law, that is, as a system of
legal norms, only if a basic norm is presupposed. The nature of
these data—the acts to be interpreted as legal acts—accounts for
the particular content of the basic norm of a particular legal
system. The basic norm is simply the expression of the necessary
presupposition of every positivistic understanding of legal data.
It is valid not as a positive legal norm—since it is not created in a
legal process, not issued or set—but as a presupposed condition
of all lawmaking, indeed, of every process of the positive law. In
formulating the basic norm, the Pure Theory of Law is not
aiming to inaugurate a new method for jurisprudence. The Pure
Theory aims simply to raise to the level of consciousness what all
jurists are doing (for the most part unwittingly) when, in
conceptualizing their object of enquiry, they reject natural law as
the basis of the validity of positive law, but nevertheless
understand the positive law as a valid system, that is, as norm,
and not merely as factual contingencies of motivation. With the
doctrine of the basic norm, the Pure Theory analyses the actual
process of the long-standing method of cognizing positive law, in
an attempt simply to reveal the transcendental logical conditions
of that method.

---

[42] Cp. § 11(b), text at n. 20.

§ 30. The Basic Norm of the State Legal System

(a) Content of the Basic Norm

Just as the essence of the law and of the community constituted by the law is most clearly revealed when their existence is in question, so it is that the significance of the basic norm becomes especially clear when a legal system, instead of being changed by legal means, is replaced by revolutionary means. A band of revolutionaries stages a violent *coup d'état* in a monarchy, attempting to oust the legitimate rulers and to replace the monarchy with a republican form of government. If the revolutionaries succeed, the old system ceases to be effective, and the new system becomes effective, because the actual behaviour of the human beings for whom the system claims to be valid corresponds no longer to the old system but, by and large, to the new system. And one treats this new system, then, as a legal system, that is to say, one interprets as legal acts the acts applying the new system, and as unlawful acts the material facts violating it. One presupposes a new basic norm, no longer the basic norm delegating lawmaking authority to the monarch, but a basic norm delegating lawmaking authority to the revolutionary government. If the revolutionaries were to fail because the system they set up remained ineffective—that is, the actual behaviour of the norm-addressees did not correspond to the new system—then the initial act of the revolutionaries would be interpreted not as the establishing of a constitution but as treason, not as the making of law but as a violation of law. And this interpretation would be based on the old system, whose validity presupposes the basic norm delegating law-creating authority to the monarch.

The question arises: what accounts for the content of the basic norm of a certain legal system? Analysing the ultimate presupposition of legal judgments shows that the content of the basic norm depends on a certain material fact, namely, the material fact creating that system to which actual behaviour (of the human beings addressed by the system) corresponds to a certain degree. To repeat: actual behaviour corresponds to the system to a certain degree. Complete correspondence, without exception, is not necessary. Indeed, there must exist the possibility of a discrepancy between the normative system and what actually takes place within its scope, for without such a possibility a normative system is meaningless; when one can assume that something will necessarily take place, one has no need to order that it happen. If a social system were to be established to which the actual behaviour of human beings always and under all conditions corresponded, then its basic norm—legitimizing at the outset all possible eventualities—would have to read, 'what ought to happen is whatever actually happens', or, 'you ought to do whatever you wish to do'. Such a system would be just as meaningless as one in which the events referred to by the system did not correspond at all to the system, but were in complete opposition to it. For that reason, a normative system to which reality no longer corresponds to a certain degree will necessarily lose its validity. The validity of a legal system governing the behaviour of particular human beings depends in a certain way, then, on the fact that their real behaviour corresponds to the legal system—depends in a certain way, as one also puts it, on the efficacy of the system. This relation of dependence, which may be characterized figuratively as the tension between 'ought' and 'is', can only be defined in terms of an upper and a lower limit. The possibility of correspondence may neither exceed a specified maximum nor fall below a specified minimum.

(b) Validity and Efficacy of the Legal System (Law and Power)

Insight into this relation of dependence can easily mislead one into identifying the validity of the legal system with its efficacy, that is, with the fact that the human behaviour referred to by the legal system corresponds to the system to a certain degree. The repeated attempt to identify validity with efficacy seems also to recommend itself because, if successful, it would substantially simplify things theoretically. But it must end in failure every time. If one claims that validity—the specific existence of the law—consists in any sort of natural reality, one is not in a position to comprehend the unique sense in which the law addresses and, precisely thereby, confronts reality; for only if reality is not identical with the validity of the law is it possible that reality either conform or fail to conform to the law. Just as one cannot, in defining validity, leave reality out of consideration, so one cannot identify validity with reality. If one replaces the concept of reality (*qua* efficacy of the legal system) with the concept of power, then the problem of the relation between the validity and the efficacy of the legal system coincides with the far more familiar problem of the relation between law and power. And then the solution is simply a theoretically exact formulation of the old truth that while the law cannot exist without power, neither is it identical with power. The law is, in terms of the theory developed here, a certain system (or organization) of power.

(c) International Law and the Basic Norm of the State Legal System

The principle that the validity of a legal system depends on a certain efficacy, more precisely, on a certain relation of correspondence, simply gives expression to the content of a positive legal norm—not a norm of the state legal system, but a norm of international law. As will be shown in greater detail below,[43] international law, by legitimizing power that is actually establishing itself, authorizes the coercive system set up by this power, that is, authorizes it in so far as it actually becomes effective. This principle of effectiveness, a principle of international law, functions as the basic norm of the various state legal systems; the constitution adopted by the first legislator, historically speaking, is valid only on the presupposition that it is effective, that reality corresponds, by and large, to the system unfolding according to constitutional provisions. Even a government that comes to power by revolutionary means or a *coup d'état* is to be regarded, in terms of international law, as a legitimate government if it is capable of securing continuous obedience to the norms it issues. What this really means is that a coercive system directly under international law is to be regarded, in terms of international law, as a legitimate, binding legal system—or, in other words, that the community constituted by such a system is to be regarded as a state—for precisely that area where the system has become continuously effective, that is, where reality corresponds, by and large, to the system.

[43] See esp. § 50(g).

The norm providing the foundation for state legal systems can be understood as a positive legal norm, and that will be the case if international law is understood as a system above the state legal systems, delegating powers to them. A basic norm, then, in the specific sense developed here—namely, a norm not issued or set, but simply presupposed—can be understood no longer as the foundation of state legal systems, but only as the basis of international law. And the principle of effectiveness, this principle of international law, can be understood only as the relative basic norm of state legal systems. If one takes the primacy of international law as one's point of departure, then the problem of the basic norm shifts its focus from state legal systems and becomes the problem of the ultimate basis of the validity of a comprehensive legal system encompassing all state legal systems. This problem will be addressed later.[44]

(d) Validity and Efficacy of a Particular Legal Norm

The validity of a legal system as a closed system of legal norms depends on the efficacy of the system. That is to say, the validity of a legal system depends on general correspondence between the system and the reality referred to in the content of the legal system taken as a whole. It does not follow that the validity of any particular legal norm, taken alone, stands in the same relation of dependence vis-à-vis the efficacy of that norm. Nor does a lack of efficacy on the part of a particular legal norm in a legal system affect the validity of the system as a whole. The inefficacious norm remains valid because and in so far as it is part of the chain of creation of a valid legal system. The question of the validity of any particular norm is answered within the system by recourse to the first constitution, which establishes the validity of all norms. If this constitution is valid, then norms issued in accordance with it must be regarded as valid. In international law, then, the principle of effectiveness has direct reference only to the first constitution of the state legal system, and thus only to the system taken as a whole, not to each and every legal norm in the system. The possibility that the validity of

---

[44] On the general question of whether the point of reference for one's 'legal world-view' is the international legal order or the individual state (the problem of 'monism vs. pluralism'), see § 50(c)–(g).

a particular legal norm might be independent of its efficacy underscores the necessity of distinguishing clearly between the concepts of validity and efficacy.

Like international law, the state legal system can, in some measure within its own territory, raise the principle of effectiveness to a principle of positive law, thereby making the validity of particular norms dependent on their efficacy. This is the case, for example, where the constitution (in the substantive sense)[45] establishes (or authorizes) custom in addition to enactment as a source of law, and then an enacted legal norm is overturned by way of custom, that is, through continuous non-application. The norm was valid until it was overturned, however, for a newly enacted statute is 'valid' even before it can become efficacious. And as long as the statute has not yet fallen into *desuetudo*,[46] non-application of the statute amounts to the material fact of an unlawful act. Thus, in these circumstances, too, validity and efficacy cannot be identified with one another.

§ 31. The Hierarchical Structure of the Legal System

(a) The Constitution

By analysing positive law raised to the level of consciousness, which is the same analysis that reveals the function of the basic norm,[47] one brings to light a special property unique to the law: the law governs its own creation. In particular, it is a legal norm that governs the process whereby another legal norm is created, and also governs—to a different degree—the content of the norm to be created. Given the dynamic character of the law, a norm is valid because and in so far as it was created in a certain way, that is, in the way determined by another norm; and this

---

[45] The constitution in the substantive or material sense is the living law, those norms actually operative in constitutional law (quite apart from whether or not they are written), as distinct from the constitution in the procedural or formal sense, the written constitutional instrument and its provisions (quite apart from whether or not they are operative). See § 31(b), text at n. 50.

[46] The doctrine of *desuetudo*—in effect 'negative customary law'—provides that where a legal norm is inefficacious over a certain period of time, it loses its validity for that reason.

[47] See § 29.

latter norm, then, represents the basis of the validity of the former norm. The relation between the norm determining the creation of another norm, and the norm created in accordance with this determination, can be visualized by picturing a higher- and lower-level ordering of norms. The norm determining the creation is the higher-level norm, the norm created in accordance with this determination is the lower-level norm. The legal system is not, then, a system of like-ordered legal norms, standing alongside one another, so to speak; rather, it is a hierarchical ordering of various strata of legal norms. Its unity consists in the chain[48] that emerges as one traces the creation of norms, and thus their validity, back to other norms, whose own creation is determined in turn by still other norms. This regress leads ultimately to the basic norm—the hypothetical basic rule—and thus to the ultimate basis of validity, which establishes the unity of this chain of creation.

The hierarchical structure of the legal system (meaning, for now, solely the single-state legal system) can be represented schematically as follows. Given that the basic norm is presupposed (this presupposition was explained above),[49] the constitution represents the highest level of the positive law, taking 'constitution' in the substantive sense of the word; and the essential function of the constitution consists in governing the organs and the process of general law creation, that is, of legislation. In addition, the constitution may determine the content of future statutes, a task not infrequently undertaken by positive-law constitutions, in that they prescribe or preclude certain content. In most cases, prescribing a certain content simply amounts to a promise of statutes to be enacted, since for reasons of legal technique alone it is not easy to attach a sanction to the failure to enact statutes having the prescribed content. Preventing statutes of a certain content is more effectively

---

[48] 'chain' ('*Zusammenhang*'). This terminology is adopted from Joseph Raz, *The Concept of a Legal System*, 2nd edn. (Oxford: Clarendon Press, 1980), 97–100, and from Adolf Julius Merkl, whose *Stufenbau* or hierarchical ordering of the legal system became part of Kelsen's own view. For Merkl, the chain (*Kette*), a 'phenomenon in the world of experience', is of help in conceptualizing the idea of a hierarchical ordering. See Merkl, 'Prolegomena einer Theorie des rechtlichen Stufenbaues', in *Gesellschaft, Staat und Recht*, ed. Alfred Verdross (n. 31 of the Introduction, above), 252–94, at 283, repr. *WS II*, 1311–61, at 1349.

[49] See §§ 28–30(a).

accomplished by the constitution. The catalogue of civil rights and liberties, a typical component of modern constitutions, is essentially a negative determination of this kind. Constitutional guarantees of equality before the law, of individual liberty, of freedom of conscience, and so on are nothing but proscriptions of statutes that treat citizens unequally in certain respects or that interfere with certain liberties. Such proscriptions can be made effective in terms of legal technique either by holding certain authorities who participate in the enactment of an unconstitutional statute (chief of state, minister) personally responsible for it, or by providing for the possibility of challenging and overturning such statutes. All of this is based on the presupposition that the ordinary statute lacks sufficient force to abrogate the constitutional provision determining the creation and the content of that statute; the presupposition is that a provision of the constitution can be amended or repealed only under more stringent conditions—for example, a majority qualified in some way, an increased quorum, and the like. That is to say, for its own amendment or repeal, the constitution must provide for procedures different from, and more demanding than, the usual legislative procedures; in addition to the procedural form applicable to statutes, there must be a specific procedural form applicable to the constitution.

(b) Legislation; the Concept of Source of Law

The next level of the hierarchical structure, one step removed from the constitution, is that of general norms created in the legislative process. The function of these norms is not only to determine the organs and the process for creating individual norms, usually issued by courts and administrative agencies, but also, above all, to determine the content of individual norms. While the main emphasis of the constitution consists in governing the process whereby statutes are enacted, with little, if any, weight given to determining their content, it is the task of legislation to determine in equal measure both the content and the creation of judicial and administrative acts. Law appearing in statutory form is both material (substantive) and formal (procedural) law. Alongside criminal law and the civil code, there is the system of criminal procedure and that of civil

procedure; alongside administrative regulations, there are statutes governing administrative procedure. The relation of the
constitution to legislation, then, is essentially the same as the
relation of the statute to adjudication or administration; the only
difference is in the ratio of procedural to substantive determination of lower-level norms by the higher-level norm. In the case of
the constitution governing legislation, the procedural element
outweighs the substantive element, whereas in the case of the
statute governing adjudication or administration, the elements
are in balance.

The hierarchical level directly governed by the constitution,
the level of general law creation, is itself usually divided into two
or more levels in the positive-law structure of state systems. Our
emphasis here is simply on the distinction between statute and
regulation, a distinction of special significance in certain
circumstances, namely: where the constitution assigns the
creation of general legal norms in principle to a popularly elected
parliament, but leaves the more detailed carrying-out of the
statutes to general norms issued by certain administrative
organs; or, where the constitution in certain exceptional cases
empowers the executive branch (instead of parliament) to issue
all necessary general norms or certain of them. General norms
stemming from an administrative agency rather than from
parliament are characterized as regulations, and they either carry
out or take the place of statutes. Such regulations are also called
statutory instruments. There is, then, a specific statutory form, just
as there is a specific constitutional form. One speaks of statutes in
the material sense, in contradistinction to statutes in the formal
sense.[50] The former characterizes every general legal norm; the
latter characterizes either the general legal norm in statutory
form—that is, the general legal norm passed by parliament and, in
accordance with the typical provisions of most constitutions,
published in a certain way—or it characterizes any content
whatever that appears in this form [for example, the statutory
instruments mentioned above]. The characterization 'statute in the
formal sense' is therefore ambiguous. The concept of statutory

---

[50] The distinction between 'material' and 'formal' adumbrated at § 30(d),
n. 45, is comparable to the distinction here.

form alone is unambiguous, a form in which not only general norms can appear but other content as well.[51]

For the sake of simplicity, the only case to be considered here is that in which the creation of general norms of the constitution—and other general norms, in accordance with the constitution—takes place by way of enactment, not custom. Enactment and custom are usually brought together in the concept of 'source of law', a metaphorical expression and therefore ambiguous. 'Source of law' may signify these two divergent methods for creating general norms—enactment, a purposeful creation brought about by central organs; and custom, an unwitting, decentralized creation by way of the legal parties themselves. Or, 'source of law' may signify the ultimate basis of the validity of the legal system, which is expressed here with the concept of the basic norm. In the broadest sense, however, 'source of law' signifies every legal norm, not only the general but also the individual legal norm, in so far as the latter *qua* objective law yields law in the subjective sense, that is, in so far as it yields a legal obligation or a legal right. Thus, a judicial decision is the source of the special obligation of one party and the corresponding right of the other party. Given its ambiguity, the expression 'source of law' seems of no use at all, and it would be well to replace the metaphor with a clear and straightforward statement of the problem to be solved in a given context. What is in question here is the general norm as 'source' of the individual norm.

(c) Adjudication

The general norm, attaching an abstractly determined consequence to an equally abstractly determined material fact, requires individualization if it is to have normative meaning at all. A material fact, determined *in abstracto* by the general norm, must be established as actually existing *in concreto*; and for this concrete case, the coercive act, prescribed likewise *in abstracto* by the general norm, must be made concrete, that is, first ordered and then realized. This multiple task is accomplished by the judicial decision, the function of adjudication or judicial power.

---

[51] 'the concept of statutory form' ('*der Begriff der Gesetzesform*'). See § 11(b), text at n. 21.

This function is not merely declaratory, although the terminology of adjudication[52] suggests otherwise, and theory occasionally assumes otherwise; the act of the court is not simply a matter of pronouncing or discovering the law already complete in the statute, the general norm. Rather, the function of adjudication is constitutive through and through; it is law creation in the literal sense of the word. That there is held to be a concrete material fact at all, which is to be linked with a specific legal consequence, and that this concrete material fact is indeed linked with the concrete legal consequence—this entire connection is created by the judicial decision. Just as the two material facts are linked at the general level by the statute, so they must be linked at the individual level by, first and foremost, the judicial decision. Thus, the judicial decision is itself an individual legal norm, the individualization or concretization of the general or abstract legal norm; it is the continuation of the process of creating law—out of the general, the individual. Only the preconceived notion that all law is contained in the general norm, the mistaken identification of law with the statute, could have obscured this insight into the judicial decision *qua* continuation of the law-creating process.

(d) Judiciary and Administration

Like adjudication, administration manifests itself as individualization and concretization of statutes, namely, as administrative regulations. Indeed, a large part of what one customarily characterizes as state administration does not differ at all, functionally speaking, from what one calls the judiciary, in so far as the administrative apparatus uses the same technique as the courts use to pursue the purposes of the state: what is socially desired (or what the legislator regards as socially desirable) is brought about in that the response to its opposite is the coercive act of an organ of the state—in other words, in that citizens are legally obligated to behave in the socially desired way. It makes no essential difference whether one speaks of the courts as protecting a person's honour by calling to account the per-

---

[52] 'terminology of adjudication' ('*Terminologie "Recht-Sprechung", "Rechts-Findung"* ' [literally 'declaring or pronouncing the law', and 'finding or discovering the law', respectively]).

petrator of dishonour, or whether one speaks of administrative agencies as ensuring a person's safety in traffic by punishing those who drive too fast. Although one speaks of the judiciary in the first example and of administration in the second, the sole difference is in the organizational status of judges, namely, in their independence (explicable only historically), an independence that administrative organs usually, but by no means always, lack. The essential agreement of the two consists in the fact that the state purpose in both examples—protecting honour and ensuring safety in traffic—is realized indirectly. A functional difference between the judiciary and administration exists only where the state purpose is realized directly through state organs, where an organ of the state fulfils a legal obligation to bring about directly what is socially desired—where it is the state itself, so to speak (that is, its organ), that builds or runs the schools and railroads, cares for the sick in hospitals, and so on. This direct administration is in fact essentially different from adjudication, which is by nature an indirect pursuit of state purposes, and therefore essentially related to indirect administration. If there is to be a functional difference between the judiciary and administration, then it is only as direct administration that the latter can be contrasted with the former. A conceptually correct systematization of legal functions calls for entirely different divisions from those found in today's familiar, historically conditioned organization of the legal apparatus, which (apart from the legislature) divides into two groups of officials, relatively isolated from one another but performing, for the most part, similar functions. Correct insight into the nature of these functions, replacing the difference between the judiciary and administration with the distinction between indirect and direct state administration, would necessarily have ramifications reaching to the organization of the legal apparatus as well.

(e) Legal Transaction; Realization of the Coercive Act

In certain fields of law—in the civil law, for example—the individualization and concretization of general norms does not proceed directly by way of acts of official organs of the state, acts like the judicial decision. With norms of the civil law that are to be applied by the courts, the legal transaction comes between the statute and the judicial decision, so to speak, thereby performing an individualizing function with regard to the conditioning material fact. Exercising powers delegated to them by statute, [private] parties set concrete norms for their own behaviour, norms that prescribe reciprocal behaviour and whose violation constitutes the material fact to be established by the judicial decision. The judicial decision then attaches to this material fact the consequence of the unlawful act, that is, it directs that the consequence be executed.

The last phase of the process of creating law, which begins with the establishing of a constitution, is the realization of the coercive act *qua* consequence of an unlawful act.

(f) Relativity of the Contrast between Creating and Applying the Law

Insight into the hierarchical structure of the legal system shows that the contrast between making or creating the law and carrying out or applying the law does not by any means have the absolute character accorded to it by traditional legal theory, where the contrast plays such a significant role. Most legal acts are acts of both law creation and law application. With each of these legal acts, a higher-level norm is applied and a lower-level norm is created. Thus, the establishing of the first constitution (an act of highest law creation) represents the application of the basic norm; legislation (the creation of general norms) represents the application of the constitution; judicial decisions and administrative acts (setting individual norms) represent the application of statutes; and the realization of coercive acts represents the application of judicial decisions and administrative directives. While the presupposition of the basic norm has the character of pure norm creation, and the coercive act has the character of pure application, everything between these limiting cases is both law creation and law application. One should note in particular that even the private law transaction is both, and it cannot be contrasted, *qua* act of law application, with legislation *qua* act of law creation—a mistake made in traditional theory. For legislation, too, like the private law transaction, is both law creation and law application.

(g) Position of International Law in the Hierarchical Structure

Let us assume that there is not just one state legal system, but that many state legal systems are valid, and that they are coordinated, and thus legally separated from each other in their spheres of validity. If one recognizes (and this will be shown below)[53] that it is positive international law that accomplishes this coordination of state legal systems and the reciprocal separation of their spheres of validity, then one must conceive of international law as a legal system above the state legal systems, bringing them together in a universal legal community. And with that, the unity of all law is assured, cognitively speaking, in one system made up of hierarchically ordered, consecutive strata of law.

(h) Conflict between Norms at Different Levels

The unity of the hierarchically constructed legal system appears to be called into question whenever a lower-level norm fails to correspond (whether in its creation or in its content) to the higher-level norm governing it, that is to say, whenever the lower-level norm runs counter to the determination underlying the hierarchical ordering of norms. The problem posed here is that of the 'norm contrary to norm',[54] namely, the unconstitutional statute, the illegal regulation (the regulation that is contrary to statute), the judicial decision or the administrative act that is contrary to statute or regulation. One has to ask how the unity of the legal system as a logically closed system of norms can remain tenable if a logical contradiction exists between two norms found at different levels of the system, if both norms—the constitution as well as the statute violating it, the statute as well as the judicial decision contradicting it—are valid. One cannot doubt, however, that this is indeed the case according to the positive law. The positive law reckons with 'law contrary to law' (illegal law),[55] and confirms its existence precisely by taking manifold precautions to prevent or, at any rate, to limit it. But in

---

[53] See § 50(b), (f)–(g).

[54] ' "norm contrary to norm" ' (*'normwidrige Norm'*). See also § 14(b), text at n. 26, and n. 55 below.

[55] ' "law contrary to law" (illegal law)' (*'rechtswidriges Recht'*). Comparable to *'normwidrige Norm'* (see n. 54 above).

so doing, for whatever reasons, in conceding the validity of even an unwanted norm *qua* law, the positive law eliminates the very quality of illegality from this law. And indeed, if the phenomenon characterized as 'norm contrary to norm'—the unconstitutional statute, the illegal judicial decision, and so on— really did amount to a logical contradiction between a higher-level norm and a lower-level norm, that would be the end of the unity of the legal system. But there is no such contradiction at all.

If, for example, an unconstitutional statute is possible—that is, a valid statute that either in the manner of its creation or in its content fails to conform to the provisions of the prevailing constitution—this can only be interpreted in one way: the constitution aims not only for the validity of the constitutional statute, but also (in some sense) for the validity of the 'unconstitutional' statute. Otherwise one could not speak of the 'validity' of the latter at all. That the constitution does aim for the validity of the so-called unconstitutional statute is shown in the fact that it prescribes not only that statutes should be created in a certain way and have (or not have) a certain content, but also that if a statute was created other than in the prescribed way or has other than the prescribed content, it is not to be regarded as null and void, but is to be valid until it is invalidated by the designated authority—say, a constitutional court—in a procedure governed by the constitution. It is of secondary importance in this connection that the constitution sometimes expressly prescribes a minimum condition—for example, promulgation in the statute book—that, if met, requires even the courts to apply as valid, until it is overturned, the norm purporting to be a statute. What is more important is that most constitutions do not provide for overturning unconstitutional statutes at all, and— leaving the validity of such statutes untouched—are satisfied simply with the possibility of holding certain authorities (chief of state or minister, for example) personally responsible for enacting the unconstitutional statute. Thus, what is termed the 'unconstitutionality' of a statute is in no way a logical contradiction between the content of the statute and the content of the constitution. Rather, this so-called 'unconstitutionality' is a condition established by the constitution for initiating a procedure that either leads to overturning the statute—valid until then and therefore constitutional—or leads to the punishment of certain authorities. The provisions of the constitution that are addressed to the creation and the content of statutes can be understood only in connection with those provisions addressed to 'violations', that is, addressed to norms issued other than in the way just prescribed, or whose content is other than the content just prescribed. Considered from this point of view, both kinds of provision form a unity. Thus, the provisions of the constitution that address legislation have the character of alternative provisions, albeit alternatives that are not accorded equal standing. The distinction between them emerges in a disqualification of the second alternative in favour of the first. And this disqualification is expressed in the fact that a statute corresponding not to the first but to the second alternative provision is declared by the constitution to be invalidatable[56] precisely because of this correspondence, or an authority is declared liable to punishment because of this statute. That a norm 'contrary to norm' can be overturned, or that an authority ought to be punished because of such a norm—therein lies not 'norm contrariety' ('unconstitutionality', 'illegality'), but what is better characterized as norm 'deficiency' or 'legal *erratum*'.

Entirely analogous is the case of the so-called illegal regulation, as well as the case of the judicial or administrative act that is contrary to statute or regulation. By way of such an act, an individual norm is created that is to be regarded as valid—and therefore lawful in terms of the statute—so long as it is not overturned, in the procedure prescribed by statute, on the basis of the claimed illegality. (An exception to this is the case of absolute nullity, where there is only the appearance of a legal norm, and thus, legally speaking, no norm at all.) The statute does not provide simply that the judicial decision and the administrative act should be created in a certain way and have a certain content; it also provides, alternatively, that even an individual norm created in another way or having another content should be valid until it is overturned, in a certain procedure, on the basis of its conflict with the first provision of the statute. Once the procedure is exhausted, or if no appropriate procedure is provided for at all, then the doctrine of finality applies, and the force of law accrues to the lower-level

---

[56] 'invalidatable' ('*vernichtbar*'). The more familiar 'nullifiable' and 'voidable' are misleading in suggesting that the overturning of the norm reaches, *eo ipso*, back to its point of issuance, rendering it null and void. Kelsen rejects nullifiability, thus understood; see below in the present section.

norm as against the higher-level norm. This means that the lower-level norm, notwithstanding the fact that its content runs counter to the higher-level norm, remains valid—indeed, it remains valid owing to a principle established by the higher-level norm itself, namely, the doctrine of finality. The meaning of the higher-level norm that provides for the creation and the content of a lower-level norm cannot be comprehended without taking account of the further provision made by the higher-level norm for the case in which its first provision is violated. Thus, the determination of the lower-level norm by the higher-level norm has the character of an alternative provision here, too, in the relation between the general norm of the statute and the individual norm of the judicial or administrative act. If the individual norm corresponds to the first of the alternatives, it is complete, adequate, on the mark; if it corresponds to the second of the alternatives, it is inferior, falling short of the mark, that is, it can be overturned owing to the claim of its deficiency. No third possibility is given, for a norm that is not invalidatable can only be definitively valid or a nullity, and a nullity is really not a norm at all but merely the appearance of one. Owing to the alternative character of the higher-level norm governing the lower-level norm, the lower-level norm is precluded from entering into a genuine logical contradiction with the higher-level norm; for a contradiction with the first of the alternative provisions into which the compound higher-level norm divides is not a contradiction with the compound norm as a whole. Furthermore, a contradiction with the first of the provisions of the higher-level norm plays no role at all until it is established by the competent authorities, reviewing the lower-level norm in the prescribed procedure. Every other opinion about an alleged contradiction is legally irrelevant. In the legal sphere, the 'contradiction' plays no role until the moment the contradicting norm is overturned. If one disregards the question of the personal responsibility of the authorities, which does not affect the norm at all, then the so-called 'norm contrariety' of a norm that is to be presupposed, for whatever reasons, as valid is simply the possibility of overturning the norm on certain grounds, its invalidatability by way of another legal act; or, this so-called 'norm contrariety' is the nullity of the norm, its negation *qua* valid norm by way of legal cognition, the dissolution of the very appearance of a valid legal norm. Either the 'norm contrary to norm' is simply invalidatable, that is, valid and thus a legal norm until its invalidation, or it is null and void, and thus not a norm at all. Normative cognition tolerates no contradiction between two norms of the same system; the possible conflict, however, between two valid norms at different levels is resolved by the law itself. The unity in the hierarchical structure of the legal system is not endangered by logical contradiction.

VI

Interpretation

§ 32. Occasion for, and the Subject-Matter of, Interpretation

The enquiry into the hierarchical structure of the legal system
has significant consequences for the problem of interpretation.
Interpretation is an intellectual activity that accompanies the
law-creating process as it moves from a higher level of the
hierarchical structure to the lower level governed by this higher
level. In the standard case, that of interpreting statutes, the
question to be answered is how, in applying the general norm
(the statute) to a concrete material fact, one is to arrive at a
corresponding individual norm (a judicial decision or an
administrative act). There is, in addition, interpretation of the
constitution in so far as the constitution is to be applied in the
legislative process, say, or in issuing emergency regulations or
other decrees stemming directly from the constitution—that is,
in so far as the constitution is to be applied at a lower level of the
hierarchy. And there is also interpretation of individual norms—
of judicial decisions, administrative directives, private law
transactions, and so on. There is, in short, interpretation of all
norms in so far as they are to be applied—that is, in so far as the
process of creating and applying the law moves from one level of
the legal system to the next.

§ 33. Relative Indeterminacy of the Lower Level of the Legal
Hierarchy

The relation between a higher and a lower level of the legal
system—as between constitution and statute, or between statute
and judicial decision—is a relation of determining or binding. As

already shown,[57] the higher-level norm governs the act whereby the lower-level norm is created (or simply governs the realization of the coercive act if pure implementation of the higher-level norm is what is called for). In governing the creation of the lower-level norm, the higher-level norm determines not only the process whereby the lower-level norm is created, but possibly the content of the norm to be created as well.

This determination, however, is never complete. The higher-level norm cannot be binding with respect to every detail of the act putting it into practice. There must always remain a range of discretion, sometimes wider, sometimes narrower, so that the higher-level norm, in relation to the act applying it (an act of norm creation or of pure implementation), has simply the character of a frame to be filled in by way of the act. Even a meticulously detailed command must leave a number of determinations to those carrying it out. If official A orders official B to arrest subject C, B must use his own discretion to decide when, where, and how he will carry out the warrant to arrest C; and these decisions depend upon external circumstances that A has not foreseen and, for the most part, cannot foresee.

§ 34. Intended Indeterminacy of the Lower Level

What emerges from the above is that every legal act applying a norm—be it an act of law creation or of pure implementation—is determined only in part by this norm and remains indeterminate for the rest. Indeterminacy can pertain to the conditioning material fact as well as to the conditioned consequence, that is, to the 'why' as well as to the 'what' of the prescribed act. Indeterminacy can be directly intended, that is, can be part of the intention of the authority issuing the higher-level norm. Thus, the issuance of a general norm always proceeds (in keeping with its nature) on the presupposition that the individual norm issued in applying the general norm will continue the process of determination, the process underlying the hierarchical ordering of legal norms. Likewise for delegation. Accompanied by a sanction for violation, a health law determines that upon

[57] See § 31(a)–(f).

outbreak of an epidemic the residents of the affected city are to take certain precautions to prevent the disease from spreading; administrative agencies are empowered to determine these precautions in various ways depending on the various diseases. Or, the criminal law provides for a fine or a gaol sentence for a specified delict; in the concrete case, the judge is left both to decide in favour of one sanction or the other and to determine its severity, for which determination an upper and a lower limit may be established in the statute itself.

§ 35. Unintended Indeterminacy of the Lower Level

Indeterminacy of the legal act can also be the unintended consequence of properties of the norm to be applied by the act in question. First of all, there is the ambiguity of a word or a phrase used in expressing the norm; the linguistic sense of the norm is not unequivocal, and whoever is to apply the norm is faced with several possible readings. The same situation exists where the organ applying the norm believes that a discrepancy between the linguistic expression of the norm and the will of the norm-issuing authority can be assumed, while the question of how the authority's will is to be discovered may well be left completely open. In any case, where the linguistic expression of the norm may be assumed not to correspond to the will of the norm-issuer, there must be the possibility of enquiring into his will by appealing to sources other than the linguistic expression itself. Traditional jurisprudence generally recognizes that the so-called will of the legislator might not correspond to the words used in the statute, and, similarly, that the intention of the parties entering into a legal transaction might not correspond to the words used in the transaction. The discrepancy between will and expression can be total, but it may be merely partial, for example, where the will of the legislator or the intention of the parties corresponds to at least one of the several possible readings of the linguistic expression of the norm. Finally, indeterminacy of the prescribed legal act can result from the fact that two norms purporting to be simultaneously valid—both contained, say, in one and the same statute—contradict one another wholly or in part. (The question of how the unity of the

legal system is to be maintained in the event of conflict between a
lower-level norm and the higher-level norm governing it—that
is, the problem of the 'norm contrary to norm'—was treated in
an earlier context.[58])

§ 36. The Norm as Frame, Encompassing Various Possibilities for Application

In all these cases of intended or unintended indeterminacy of the
lower level, various possibilities for applying the higher-level
norm suggest themselves. The legal act applying the legal norm
can be made to correspond to one or another of the several
possible readings of the norm. Or it can be made to correspond
to the norm-issuer's will, however discovered, or to the
expression he chooses. Or, in the case of two norms contradicting each other, the legal act can be made to correspond to one or
the other of them, or it can be so fashioned that decisions are
taken as if the norms abrogated one another. In all these cases,
the norm to be applied is simply a frame within which various
possibilities for application are given, and every act that stays
within this frame, in some possible sense filling it in, is in
conformity with the norm.

If 'interpretation' is understood as discovering the meaning of
the norm to be applied, its result can only be the discovery of the
frame that the norm to be interpreted represents and, within this
frame, the cognition of various possibilities for application.
Interpreting a statute, then, leads not necessarily to a single
decision as the only correct decision, but possibly to a number of
decisions, all of them of equal standing (measured solely against
the norm to be applied), even if only a single one of them
becomes, in the act of the judicial decision, positive law. That a
judicial decision is based on a statute means in truth simply that
the decision stays within the frame the statute represents, means
simply that the decision is one of the individual norms possible
within the frame of the general norm, not that it is the only
individual norm possible.

In traditional jurisprudence, however, more is expected from
interpretation than simply the discovery of the frame for the

[58] See § 31(h).

prescribed legal act. The additional task to be accomplished, which traditional jurisprudence is inclined to see even as the main task of interpretation, is the development of a method for filling in the discovered frame correctly. The familiar theory of interpretation would have us believe that, invariably, when the statute is applied in the concrete case, it can provide only *one* correct decision, and that the 'correctness' of this decision—its correctness in terms of the positive law—is based on the statute itself. Traditional theory depicts the process of arriving at this interpretation as though it were an intellectual act of clarification or understanding, as though the interpreter had only to set into motion his mind and not his will, as though by sheer mental activity he could choose from among the existing possibilities one that corresponds to the positive law, and so make a correct choice in terms of the positive law.

§ 37. The So-Called Methods of Interpretation

From the standpoint of the positive law, however, there is no criterion on the basis of which one of the possibilities given within the frame of the norm to be applied could be favoured over the other possibilities. In terms of the positive law, there is simply no method according to which only one of the several readings of a norm could be distinguished as 'correct'— assuming, of course, that several readings of the meaning of the norm are possible in the context of all other norms of the statute or of the legal system. In spite of every effort, traditional jurisprudence has not yet found an objectively plausible way to settle the conflict between will and expression. Every method of interpretation developed thus far invariably leads merely to a possible result, never to a single correct result. From the standpoint of the positive law, it is a matter of complete indifference whether one neglects the text in order to stick to the legislator's presumed will, or strictly observes the text in order to avoid concerning oneself with the legislator's (usually problematic) will. Given the case where two simultaneously valid norms contradict one another, each of the three logical possibilities for application mentioned above[59] has the very same standing in

[59] See § 36, at the fourth sentence.

terms of the positive law. It is futile to try to establish 'legally' one possibility by excluding the others. Both familiar means of interpretation, *argumentum a contrario*[60] and analogy, are worthless, if only because they lead to opposite results and there is no criterion for deciding when to use one or the other. Even the principle of the so-called balancing of interests is merely a formulation of the problem here, and not a solution. It does not supply the objective standard according to which competing interests can be compared with one another as a means of settling conflicts of interest. In particular, this standard is not to be drawn from the norm to be interpreted, or from the statute containing the norm, or from the legal system as a whole, as the doctrine of the so-called balancing of interests suggests it can be. The necessity of an 'interpretation' arises precisely because the norm to be applied—or the system of norms—leaves open various possibilities, which is really to say that neither the norm nor the system of norms provides a decision as to which of the interests involved is of greater value. This decision, this ranking of interests, is left instead to a future act of norm creation—to the judicial decision, for example.

§ 38. Interpretation as Act of Cognition or Act of Will

The notion underlying the traditional theory of interpretation is that in so far as the prescribed legal act is indeterminate, the determination not provided by the applicable higher-level norm can be arrived at through some sort of cognition of existing law. This self-contradictory notion flies in the face of the very presupposition that there can be interpretation at all. For if there can be an interpretation of a norm, then the question as to which is the 'correct' choice from among the possibilities given within the frame of the norm is hardly a question of cognition directed to the positive law; it is a problem not of legal theory but of legal policy.[61] The task of getting the correct judicial decision or the correct administrative act out of the statute is essentially the

[60] The *argumentum a contrario*, deployed as a parry to the argument by analogy, in effect says: because the statute expressly specifies (only) *A* as falling within its scope, then *B*, *C*, *D*, etc. do not fall within its scope, notwithstanding their similarity to *A*.

[61] 'legal policy' ('*Rechtspolitik*'). See §1, n.2, above, and Supplementary Note 2, in appendix I.

same task as creating the correct statute within the framework of the constitution. Just as one cannot get correct statutes out of the constitution by way of interpretation, so likewise one cannot get correct judicial decisions out of the statute by way of interpretation. Certainly there is a difference between these two cases, but it is only a quantitative and not a qualitative difference, consisting simply in the fact that the legislator is far less bound materially than the judge—in other words, the legislator enjoys far greater independence in creating law. But even the judge creates law, even he is relatively independent in this capacity. And precisely for this reason, it is a function of will to arrive at the individual norm in the process of applying a statute, provided that the frame of the general norm is filled in thereby. 'Theoretical' commentaries supposedly assisting in applying a statute are in fact thoroughly political, making suggestions for the legislator to consider, attempting to influence the creative function of the courts and administrative agencies. In applying a statute, there may well be room for cognitive activity beyond discovering the frame within which the act of application is to be confined; this is not cognition of the positive law, however, but cognition of other norms, which can now make their way into the law-creating process, the norms, namely, of morality, of justice—social value-judgments customarily characterized with the catch-phrases 'welfare of the people', 'public interest', 'progress', and so on. From the standpoint of the positive law, nothing can be said about their validity and whether or not they can be identified. From this vantage-point, all such deter-minations can only be characterized negatively: they are determina-tions that do not stem from the positive law itself. In relation to the positive law, the legal act is free of such constraints, that is, the authority called upon to act is free to do so according to his own discretion unless the positive law itself authorizes some metalegal norm such as morality, justice, and so on. This norm, however, would be transformed thereby into a norm of the positive law.

§ 39. The Illusion of Legal Certainty

The view that interpretation is cognition of the positive law, and, as such, is a way of deriving new norms from prevailing norms, is the foundation of the so-called jurisprudence of concepts,[62] which the Pure Theory of Law also rejects. The Pure Theory demolishes the view that norms could be created by way of cognition, a view that arises in the end from the need to imagine the law as a fixed system governing every aspect of human behaviour, in particular the activity of law-applying organs, above all the courts. Their function—and thus interpretation too—is to be seen only as the discovery of norms that already exist, and thus are simply to be uncovered in a particular way. The illusion of legal certainty is what traditional legal theory, wittingly or not, is striving to maintain.

§ 40. The Problem of Gaps

Interpretation is given a special role to play in filling gaps in the law. Genuine gaps, however, do not exist. A genuine gap would mean that a legal dispute could not be settled in accordance with prevailing norms because the statute—as one says—lacks a provision addressing the case, and therefore cannot be applied. Every legal dispute consists in one party making a claim against another party, and the decision granting or rejecting the claim depends on whether or not the statute—that is, a valid norm to be applied in the concrete case—establishes the claimed legal obligation. Since there is no third possibility, a decision can always be made, and, indeed, can always be made on the basis of the statute, that is, by applying the statute. Even a decision rejecting the claim is made by appeal to the prevailing legal system. By imposing obligations on human beings to behave in particular ways, the legal system guarantees them liberty outside those obligations. A may demand that B behave in a way not established as obligatory by the prevailing legal system, but the legal system grants B the 'right' to forbear from this behaviour, a 'right' in terms of legally guaranteed liberty. The legal system

---

[62] 'jurisprudence of concepts' ('*Begriffsjurisprudenz*'). The early 19th-century view, associated above all with Puchta and the early Rudolf von Jhering, is that legal science, 'identifying legal norms as systematically related to one another', brings legal norms to light 'as the product of a scientific deduction (*einer wissenschaftlichen Deduktion*)'. Puchta, *Cursus der Institutionen*, 10th edn., vol. i (§ 20 above, n. 37), 22. For some details on Jhering's *Begriffsjurisprudenz*, see Supplementary Note 7, in appendix I.

embraces not only the principle that one is obligated to behave in a certain way (in so far as behaving in the opposite way is set as condition for the specific consequence of an unlawful act), but also the principle that where one is not obligated to do or to forbear from doing, there one is free. It is this negative norm that is applied in a decision rejecting a claim directed to behaviour not established as obligatory.

If in certain cases one nevertheless speaks of a 'gap', this does not mean, as the expression misleadingly suggests, that a decision is logically impossible for want of a norm. Rather, it simply means that the decision granting or rejecting a claim, while logically possible, is felt to be too impractical or too unjust by the authority called upon to take the decision, that is, called upon to apply the statute. Indeed, the decision is felt to be so impractical or so unjust that the authority is inclined to assume that the legislator did not consider this case at all, and that, if he had, he would have decided it differently than it would have to be decided on the basis of the statute. Whether or not the authority's assumption is correct probably cannot be shown; but in the face of the constitutionally established obligation to apply the norm that the legislator actually issued, it is irrelevant that he presumably would have issued a different norm had he considered the case at hand. Even the statute that is bad in the view of the law-applying authority is to be applied, quite apart from the fact that what some regard as bad appears to others to be good. The so-called 'gap', then, is nothing but the difference between the positive law and a system held to be better, more just, more nearly right. Only by placing this 'better' system alongside the system of positive law and thereby ascertaining the latter's shortcomings, only thus can one claim something like a 'gap'. The fact that it cannot be filled by way of interpretation is obvious as soon as one recognizes its nature. The function of interpretation here is not to bring about the application of the norm to be interpreted; on the contrary, its function is to eliminate the norm to be interpreted, in order to replace it with a norm that is better, more just, more nearly right—in short, the norm desired by the authority applying it. Under the pretext that the original norm is being supplemented to make up for its deficiencies, it is overturned in the course of being applied and is replaced by a new norm. This fiction is useful particularly where legal revision of general norms is, for whatever reasons, difficult or impossible—because, say, customary law is involved, which cannot be modified in a rational process at all, or because the prevailing statutes are regarded as inviolable or of divine origin, or because the legislative apparatus is, for whatever other reasons, difficult or impossible to set into motion.

§ 41. So-Called Technical Gaps

Alongside gaps proper, one occasionally distinguishes technical gaps. Technical gaps are regarded as possible even by those who, from a positivistic standpoint, deny the existence of genuine gaps; and the filling of technical gaps by way of interpretation is declared admissible. Technical gaps are said to exist where the legislator fails to regulate something that he would have to regulate to make technically possible the application of a statute. What is characterized as a technical gap, however, is either a gap in the original sense of the word—that is, a difference between positive law and desired law—or it is that indeterminacy that stems from the frame-like character of the norm. An example of the first alternative: a statute establishes the binding force of a sale, but—as one puts it—determines nothing on the question of who bears the risk if the item sold is ruined, before delivery, through no fault of either party. However, it is not that the legislator determines 'nothing' on the question. Rather, it is that he does not determine that the seller is freed of the obligation to deliver the goods or to provide a substitute, a determination obviously regarded as desirable by the individual claiming a 'gap' here, but a determination that by no means has to be imagined in order to render the statute applicable. Because the statute makes no exceptions to the seller's obligation to deliver the goods (no exceptions in the case mentioned here either), it determines that the seller bears the risk. An example of the second alternative with respect to what is characterized as a technical gap: a statute determines that an agency is to be created by way of an election, but does not regulate the election procedure. This means that any sort of election whatever is lawful, whether it be based on proportional or majority vote, whether it be conducted in public or in secret, and so on. The authority empowered to carry out the election can use his own discretion to determine the election procedure; in other words, the determination of the election procedure is left to a lower-level norm. Another example: a statute determines that in order to take action, a committee must be convened by its chairman; at the same time, the statute determines that the committee itself is to elect its chairman, but determines nothing about how the committee is to assemble in case there is no chairman. If one cannot wrest from this norm the sense that, in case there is no chairman, any sort of assembly whatever is lawful, its meaning can only be that in this case, too, the committee is to be convened by its chairman—which means that the committee cannot function lawfully at all. Even here, however, no 'gap' exists. For the statute does provide that the committee is to be convened by its chairman, [and the provision stands] even when the committee has no chairman. If the statute prescribed nothing for this case, then any sort of assembly whatever would be lawful. To be sure, the statute determines something nonsensical here, but that can happen; statutes are, after all, the handiwork of human beings. A norm can even be lacking in meaning altogether, and then no interpretation can wrest meaning from it. For one cannot extract from a norm by way of interpretation what the norm never had.

§ 42. The Legislator's Theory of Gaps

Theoretically, then, there are no gaps in the law. The legislator, however, influenced by a mistaken theory, may nevertheless presuppose the existence of 'gaps', even though these are not what he himself perhaps considers them to be. The legislator may—and indeed frequently does—establish provisions that speak to cases where no decision can be derived from the statute, provisions like [article 7] of the Austrian Civil Code[63] and article

---

[63] Austrian General Civil Code, art. 7: 'If a case cannot be decided either from the language or from the natural sense of the statute, then consideration must be given to similar cases decided with certainty in the statutes, and to the basis of other statutes related to the statute in question. Should the case still remain doubtful, then it must be decided with reference to the carefully compiled and well-considered circumstances, this in accordance with the principles of natural law.' (Kelsen's reference in the text is to article 6, but this is clearly a

1 of the Swiss Civil Code.[64] If, as in the latter, the statute
instructs the judge to decide in case of a 'gap' as he would decide
qua legislator, this amounts to empowering the judge, in cases
where he considers application of the statute unacceptable, to
decide according to his own discretion instead of on the basis of
the statute. The good legislator is not in a position to dispense
with what might well be a necessary correction of his statute, for
since he must reckon from the beginning with material facts that
he has not foreseen and cannot foresee, he can only address his
general norms to the ordinary run of cases. Precisely for this
reason, he cannot even describe those cases where he intends that
the law-applying authority stand in for him; were he able to
describe such cases, he would have no need for a stand-in. The
legislator has no alternative but to leave the selection of cases to
the law-applying authority, and to take the unavoidable risk that
the latter will decide *qua* 'delegated legislator' even cases where
the original legislator would wish to have his statute applied.
The risk here, of course, is that questions will arise about the
principle of lawfulness in the application of those general norms
that are issued expressly to be applied by courts and administrative agencies, and thus, questions will arise about the very
validity of those general norms. The full import of law creation
threatens to shift from the general to the individual level, that is,
from the legislator to the law-applying authority. To minimize
this risk as much as possible, the empowerment to circumvent
the statute is formulated in such a way that the law-applying
authority is not made aware of the extraordinary power that is
actually being delegated to him. He is to believe that he may
forbear from applying the statute only in those cases where it
cannot be applied because it is in and of itself impossible to
apply. He is to believe that he is free [to decide according to his

typographical error or a slip; for article 6, addressed to 'plain meaning' and
legislative intent, speaks to cases where a decision can be drawn from the
statute—precisely the opposite of Kelsen's present context, in which the
statutory provision speaks to 'cases where no decision can be derived from the
statute'.)

[64] Swiss Civil Code, art. 1: 'The statute applies to all legal questions for
which, in its terms or its exposition, it contains a provision. If no directive can be
derived from the statute, then the judge shall decide in accordance with
customary law or, failing that, the rule that he as legislator would adopt. He
should be guided therein by established doctrine and tradition.'

own discretion] only where he himself is to function as legislator, but not free with respect to when he is to stand in for the legislator. The fact that he is in truth free even in this latter respect is concealed from him by the fiction of the 'gap'. It is the legislator's intention that this formulation, wittingly or unwittingly false, have the effect that the law-applying authority makes only the most sparing use of his conceded freedom not to apply the statute in a concrete case. For to the authority applying a statute, only the greatest divergence between the statute and his own sense of the law will appear to be a real 'gap', that is, a case that the legislator himself did not wish to regulate and that the statute therefore does not regulate; the logical premisses are lacking, then, for the conclusion from general to particular that is represented in every act of law application. The formulation of so-called 'gaps in the law' is typically ideological, depicting the application of a statute as logically impossible, when—judged according to the discretion of the law-applying authority—it may simply be politically impractical.

VII

The Methods of Creating Law

§ 43. Form of Law and Form of State

The doctrine of the hierarchical structure of the legal system comprehends the law in motion, in the constantly regenerating process of its self-creation. It is a dynamic theory of law—in contradistinction to a static theory, which seeks to comprehend the law (its validity, its sphere of validity, and so on) apart from the process of its creation, and simply as a system already created. Problems of a legal dynamic are centred on the question of the various methods of creating law, the question of the forms of law. If one recognizes that the essential function of the legal norm is to impose on a human being an obligation to behave in a certain way (in that it links the opposite behaviour with a coercive act, the so-called consequence of an unlawful act), then the decisive point in evaluating the creation of the legal norm is whether the human being to be obligated by the norm—its subject—participates in its creation or not. In other words, the question is whether the obligation is imposed with or without the subject's consent, perhaps even against his will. The difference here is usually characterized as the opposition between autonomy and heteronomy. It is a difference that legal theory traditionally makes use of in the field of public law, where it turns up as the difference between democracy and autocracy, or between republic and monarchy, providing the familiar classification of the forms of state. What is understood as the form of state, however, is simply a particular case of the form of law in general, namely, the method of creating law at the highest hierarchical level of the legal system, the level of the constitution. It is the constitutionally governed method of creating general norms that is captured in the concept of the form of state. If, however, one understands by the form of state the constitution

alone as the form for legislation, for creating general legal
norms, and if, therefore, in the concept of the form of state, one
identifies the state with the constitution *qua* form for creating
general legal norms, then one is going along with the familiar
notion of the law as simply a system of general norms. And one
fails to take into account the fact that the individualization of
general legal norms, the progression from abstract to concrete
legal norm, must also fall within the bounds of the legal system.
Identifying the form of state with the constitution is thoroughly
in keeping with the preconception that the law is contained in
the statute. But the problem of the form of state as a question
about the method of creating law arises not only at the level of
the constitution, and thus not only with reference to legislation.
The problem arises at all levels of law creation, and in particular
with reference to the various cases of individual norm issuance—
administrative act, judicial decision, private law transaction.

§ 44. Private and Public Law

As a particularly characteristic example of the problem with
reference to the issuance of individual norms, the distinction
between private and public law is cited, a distinction fundamental to the systematization of modern legal science. It is well
known that no one has yet succeeded in arriving at a fully
satisfactory statement of the difference between private and
public law. The most widely disseminated view turns on a
classification of legal relations, with private law representing a
relation between coordinate subjects of equal standing legally,
and public law representing a relation between a superordinate
and a subordinate subject—between two subjects, then, one of
which is of higher standing legally than the other. The typical
public law relation is that between state and citizen. One
characterizes private law relations also as legal relations *per se*,
'legal' relations in the literal, narrower sense of the word, in
contrast with public law relations *qua* 'power' relations. Thus,
the very distinction between private and public law tends to take
on the import of an opposition between law and power (non-
legal or only half-legal power), the opposition, especially,
between law and state. If one looks more closely at the higher

standing accorded to certain subjects, their superior ranking vis-à-vis other subjects, one sees that it really consists in a distinction between law-creating material facts. And the telling difference is the same as that underlying the classification of the forms of state. The higher legal standing attributed to the state—that is, to its organs in relation to citizens—consists in the fact that the legal system empowers those human beings who are qualified as organs of the state (or certain of them, so-called authorities) to impose obligations on citizens by means of a unilateral expression of will (a directive or command). Typical of the public law relation is the administrative directive, an individual norm issued by an administrative organ, whereby the addressee of the norm is legally obligated to behave in accordance with the directive. Typical of the private law relation is the legal transaction, especially the contract, that is, an individual norm created by contract, whereby the parties entering into the contract are legally obligated to behave in certain reciprocal ways. Here the parties who are subject to obligation participate in creating the norm that imposes obligations, and therein lies the essence of the contractual creation of law. In the case of the public law administrative directive, however, the party who is subject to obligation plays no role whatever in creating the norm that imposes obligations. While the latter case is typical of the autocratic creation of norms, the private law contract represents a decidedly democratic method of creating law. It is completely fitting, then, that even the earliest theorists characterized the sphere of the legal transaction as the sphere of private autonomy.

§ 45. Ideological Significance of the Dualism of Private and Public Law

Suppose that one conceives of the telling difference between private and public law as the difference between two methods of creating law, and that one recognizes precisely the same legal acts both in private law transactions and in so-called public acts of the state. And suppose, above all, that one appreciates that the expression of will constituting the law-creating material fact in both cases is simply the continuation of the process of forming the will of the state, that what is accomplished in both the private law transaction and the authoritative directive is simply the individualization of a general norm—of a provision of the civil code in the one case, of an administrative regulation in the other. It will seem not at all so paradoxical, then, that from the universalistic standpoint of the Pure Theory of Law, always focused on the whole of the legal system *qua* so-called will of the state, both the private law transaction and the authoritative directive are perceived as acts of the state, that is, as material facts of law creation that are imputable to the unity of the legal system. The Pure Theory of Law thereby relativizes the opposition between private and public law, transforming it into an intra-systemic opposition, from the absolute, extra-systemic opposition of traditional legal theory, that is, from the difference between law and non-law, between law and state. And the Pure Theory proves itself as a science by breaking down the ideology, too, that is linked with absolutizing the opposition between private and public law. For to represent the opposition as an absolute opposition between law and power (or at least between law and state power) is to create the illusion that in the field of public law—in particular, in the politically significant fields of constitutional and administrative law—the principle of law[65] would not obtain in the same sense or with the same intensity as in the field of private law, regarded, so to speak, as the proper realm of the law. Public law, as distinct from private law, would be dominated not so much by strict law as by the state interest, the public welfare, which would have to be realized whatever the circumstances. Thus, the relation between a general norm and the organ applying it would be different in the private and public law fields; in private law, the application of statutes to concrete cases would be constrained, bound by the statute, while in public law, realization of the state purpose would be unhampered, constrained merely by the framework of the statute. In an emergency, that is, in the case of a so-called national state of emergency, the realization of the state purpose could even go against the statute.

However, critical investigation reveals no foundation in the positive law for this entire distinction—not, at any rate, in so far as it is saying more than simply that the activity of legislative, executive, and administrative organs is subject, as a rule, to

---

[65] 'principle of law' ('*Rechtsprinzip*').

fewer statutory constraints than the activity of the courts, that the positive law usually concedes a narrower range of discretion to the courts. Moreover, in claiming that the field of public 'law', the realm of the state's existence, is independent of the law, the doctrine of an essential difference between private and public law becomes entangled in the contradiction of claiming that independence from the law is a principle of law, a specific characteristic of public law. At best, the doctrine could speak of two fields of law, differently structured in terms of technique, but it cannot speak in absolute terms of an essential opposition between law and state. This logically untenable dualism has only ideological significance, not theoretical significance. Developed from constitutional doctrine, this dualism is supposed to secure the independence of the executive branch of government and its subordinate administrative apparatus, independence derived, so to speak, from the nature of things; this is not independence from the law—which would be impossible—but independence from the statute, from the general norms created by the people's representatives or with their substantial participation. It is independence from the statute not only in the sense that far-reaching statutory constraints on the executive and administrative organs are declared contradictory to the nature of their respective functions, but also in the sense that statutory constraints, where they nevertheless do exist, are declared vulnerable to being ignored if need be. And this bias—given the habitual opposition between the executive branch and parliament—is found in democracies as well as in constitutional monarchies.

Representing as absolute the opposition between private and public law also creates the illusion that the field of public law alone—above all, the fields of constitutional and administrative law—is the domain of political power, which is totally excluded from the field of private law. As shown in an earlier context,[66] this entire opposition between 'private' and 'political' does not exist with reference to subjective rights; private law rights are political in the same sense as those rights that are usually characterized as political rights, because both—although in different ways—guarantee participation in forming the will of the state, which is really participation in political power. To

[66] See § 24(c).

distinguish in principle between a private non-political sphere of the law and a public political sphere is to obscure the fact that the 'private' law created in the contract is no less the arena of political power than the public law created in legislation and administration. What we call private law, seen from the standpoint of its function—*qua* part of the legal system—in the fabric of the law as a whole, is simply a particular form of law, the form corresponding to the capitalistic economic system of production and distribution; its function, then, is the eminently political function of exercising power. Another form of law would suit a socialistic economic system, not the autonomous, democratic form represented by present private law, but—presumably—a heteronomous, autocratic form closer to the form of our present administrative law. Whether that would be a more satisfying or more just form of regulation remains an open question here. The Pure Theory of Law does not aim to decide the question, and cannot decide it.

VIII

Law and State

§ 46. Traditional Dualism of Law and State

What is most salient in the opposition that traditional legal theory assumes between private and public law is a powerful dualism dominating modern legal science and thus our thinking on social matters generally—the dualism, namely, of law and state. In traditional legal and political theory, the state, being essentially different from the law, is contrasted with the law, while at the same time it is claimed to be essentially legal in character; this dualism is the result when traditional theory attributes to the state an existence independent of the legal system, while at the same time regarding the state as a subject of legal obligations and rights, that is, as a [legal] person.

Just as the theory of private law assumed at the outset that the legal personality of the individual logically and temporally precedes the objective law (the legal system), so the theory of public law assumes that the state, as a collective unity that is originally the subject of will and of action, exists independently of, and even prior to, the law. But the state goes on to fulfil its historic mission, so theory has it, by creating law, 'its' law, the objective legal system, in order to subject itself to that system, in order to use its own law to impose obligations on, and to grant rights to, itself. Thus, the state—essentially metalegal in character, some kind of powerful macro-anthropos or social organism—is a presupposition of the law and is at the same time a legal subject presupposing the law because beholden to the law, because obligated and granted rights by the law. This notorious 'two-sides' and self-obligating theory of the state,[67] in spite of the blatant contradictions with which it is repeatedly charged, holds its own with singular tenacity in the face of all objections.

[67] ' "two-sides" and self-obligating theory of the state' (*Zwei-Seiten- und Selbstverpflichtungs-Theorie des Staates*). The allusion is to Georg Jellinek's

§ 47. Ideological Function of the Dualism of Law and State

Traditional legal and political theory cannot dispense with this
theory of the state, cannot dispense with the dualism of law and
state that is manifest in the theory. For this dualism performs an
ideological function of extraordinary significance, impossible to
overestimate. The state must be imagined as a person, different
from the law, so that the law can justify the state, which creates
and subjects itself to the law. And the law can justify the state
only if the law is presupposed as a system essentially different
from the state, a system in opposition to the original nature of
the state, namely power, and thus in some sense a 'right' or just
system. From a naked fact of power, the state becomes the
Rechtsstaat,[68] which justifies itself by making law. To the extent
that a metaphysico-religious legitimization of the state ceases to
be effective, this theory of the *Rechtsstaat* inevitably becomes the
sole possible justification of the state. When this 'theory' claims
the state to be a legal person, it turns the state into an object of
legal cognition, an object of enquiry for the theory of public law.
But it emphasizes at the same time that the state cannot be
comprehended legally because the state *qua* power is essentially
different from the law. This contradiction does not undermine
the 'theory'; contradictions are inherent in ideological theories,
and do not amount to a serious impediment. For the aim of
ideologies is not really to expand cognition, but to determine
will, the aim is not so much to comprehend the essence of the
state, as to strengthen its authority.

'two-sides' theory of the state and to his theory of the 'self-limitation' of the state.
On the former, see Jellinek, *Allgemeine Staatslehre*, 3rd edn. (Berlin: O. Häring,
1914, many reprints), 10–12, 136–9, 174–83; on the latter, see ibid. 367–75.
For unusually vigorous criticism of the 'two-sides' theory, see Kelsen, *Der
soziologische und der juristische Staatsbegriff* (Tübingen: J. C. B. Mohr, 1922,
repr. Aalen: Scientia, 1962), 114–20; for criticism of the 'self-limiting' theory,
see ibid. 132–6.

   [68] '*Rechtsstaat*' may be translated as 'state or government based on the rule of
law'. In contradistinction to the principle of law (see § 45, text at n. 65), Kelsen
regards the notion of the *Rechtsstaat* as ideologically encumbered. See also
§ 48(*e*).

§ 48. The Identity of Law and State

(a) State as Legal System

Cognition that is free of ideology, and thus free of all metaphysics and mysticism, can grasp the essence of the state only by comprehending this social structure as a system of human behaviour. A closer look shows it to be a coercive social system, which must be identical with the legal system since the very same coercive acts distinguish both systems, and since one and the same social community cannot be constituted by two different systems. The state, then, is a legal system. Not every legal system, however, is characterized as a state; this characterization is used only where the legal system establishes certain organs—whose respective functions reflect a division of labour—for creating and applying the norms forming the legal system. When the legal system has achieved a certain degree of centralization, it is characterized as a state.

In the primitive, pre-state legal community, general legal norms are created by way of custom, that is, by way of the practices of each and every party to the law. And in this primitive state, there are no central courts for issuing individual norms either, or, in particular, for enforcing them with coercive acts. Ascertaining the material fact of an unlawful act and realizing its consequences are both left to those whose interests are violated—interests that are protected, then, in precisely this way by the legal system. The son is to take revenge on his father's murderer and the murderer's family; the creditor himself is to take the defaulting debtor in hand and to settle accounts, by, say, attaching the debtor's property. These are primitive forms of punishment and enforcement, material facts brought about by members of the community who, because they are duly empowered by the legal system, are acting as organs of the legal system and of the community constituted by that system. By virtue of such empowerment, these coercive acts can be linked by imputation to the community, and thus it is the community that is responding to unlawful acts with coercive acts, which do not themselves count as unlawful acts because they are linked by imputation to the community. It is only over the course of a long-term evolution that central organs develop out of the process of a social division of labour; characteristically, judicial and enforcement organs develop much earlier than lawmaking organs. However enormous this step may be from the standpoint of legal technique, the difference between decentralized and centralized legal systems, between primitive and state legal communities, is none the less simply a quantitative difference, not a qualitative one.

So long as there is no legal system higher than the state legal system, the state itself is the highest, the sovereign legal system or legal community. The territorial and material spheres of validity of this legal system are in fact limited, because the state coercive system itself restricts its own validity to a certain area and to certain objects—that is, it does not claim validity everywhere, at least not substantively, and does not purport to cover all human relations. To say, however, that the state is the sovereign legal system means, in particular, that it has the capacity, unrestricted by any higher legal system, to extend its validity territorially as well as materially. This is usually characterized as absolute sovereignty. But as soon as the international legal system rises above the legal systems of the individual states, the state can no longer be understood as the sovereign legal system; it can be understood only as the highest legal system relatively speaking, that is, the highest legal system save for international law, a legal system directly under international law. Before the state can be qualified further, its relation to the international legal system must be accounted for. Like the pre-state legal community, the supra-state community constituted by the international legal system is insufficiently centralized to be considered a state.

(b) State as Problem of Legal Imputation

That the state is a legal system—qualified in a certain way and distinguished from other kinds of legal systems simply quantitatively, not qualitatively—is also seen in the fact that the state's every expression of existence, its every act, can only appear as a legal act, as an act creating or applying legal norms. An act of a human being is an act of state only because it is qualified as such by a legal norm. From the standpoint of the individual acts of state that make up the state *qua* dynamic phenomenon, the problem of the state is a problem of imputation. Every act of state is first of all simply an act of a human being, and the problem of imputation is expressed in the question of why a certain human act is imputed not to the acting human being himself but to a subject imagined, so to speak, behind the human being. The only possible criterion for this imputation proves to be the legal norm. Because and in so far as the material fact of a human act is established in a specific way in a legal norm, it can be related to the unity of the legal system containing the qualifying norm. The state *qua* subject of the acts of state, which is really the state *qua* person, is nothing other than the personification of a system that, as a legal system, is a coercive system; and it is precisely as this coercive system alone that the state can be comprehended. The imputation to the state *qua* person turns the imputed material fact into an act of state, and qualifies the human being who brings about this material fact as an organ of the state. Thus, the legal person of the state exhibits the very same character as every other legal person. Like these others, the legal person of the state—*qua* expression of the unity of a legal system[69]—is a point of imputation, which the cognizing theorist, his intellect striving after imagery, is all too inclined to hypostatize, to posit as real, concrete, in order to imagine behind the legal system something essentially different from it, namely, the state.

(c) State as Bureaucracy

As soon as the legal system has surmounted the primitive stage of complete decentralization, as soon as organs functioning along lines that reflect a division of labour have developed to create and to apply legal norms—in particular, to carry out coercive acts—then, from the mass of the citizenry, the norm subjects, there emerges a distinct group of individuals qualified in a specific way as organs. (This is not, incidentally, complete centralization, since certain functions of creating and applying the law always remain decentralized.) It is essential to this centralization that the organ's function, reflecting a division of

[69] 'qua expression of the unity of a legal system' ('*als Ausdruck der Einheit eine Rechtsordnung*'), rendering 'a legal system' (nominative case) as 'of a legal system' ('*einer Rechtsordnung*', genitive case). See e.g. § 25(b), (d).

labour, be generally established as a legal obligation, that its non-performance be subject to a specific consequence of an unlawful act, the sanction of disciplinary action; and it is essential that the function gradually take on professional and salaried status. The state organ functioning along lines that reflect a division of labour becomes—as bearer of the centralized legal function—a state official, which is an organ legally qualified in a specific way. This development, linked to the transition from a natural to a money economy, presupposes the formation of a state treasury, of central assets, whose acquisition and disbursement, increase and decrease, are legally regulated in a particular way, and from which the salaries of state officials are paid and the costs of their activities are financed. The state, acting through these officials, carries out in particular what was characterized above[70] as direct state administration, the direct pursuit of state purposes. To say that it is the state and not a private party that builds a school or runs a railroad is to say that the human being performing this function is qualified in a specific way. The apparatus comprising official organs of the state—the bureaucracy—is key to the evolution from judicial state to administrative state. Of course, one must not overlook the fact that the administrative state, too, is a coercive system. The administrative state is that state whose officials directly pursue state purposes by directly bringing about what is socially desired. They do not confine themselves to creating and applying norms according to which citizens (not officials) are obligated to behave in the socially desired way because officials respond with a coercive act against citizens who behave in the opposite way. Rather, direct state administration is brought about in the same way, legally speaking, as the socially desired behaviour of citizens: namely, as a legal obligation of state officials. That is to say, the legal system directs state organs to respond with a coercive act against those state organs behaving contrary to their obligations. The state *qua* coercive apparatus encompasses the state *qua* administrative apparatus.

With the development of a system of organs functioning along lines that reflect a division of labour, the concept of state organ in the narrower sense—*qua* official, an organ legally qualified in

[70] See § 31(d).

a specific way—confronts the concept of citizen *qua* private party. Ordinary language generally restricts the characterization 'state organ' to the official. A citizen who is not an official may create legally binding norms in a legal transaction duly authorized by the legal system, but he is not called a 'state organ', although his function is the same as that of an administrative official who issues a regulation. Ordinary language, however, is far from consistent. The private party who functions as a parliamentary elector, as well as the elected party and the parliament made up of the elected—none of these is specifically qualified as an official, yet all count in full measure as 'state organs'; and obviously this is so simply because they perform a legal function. Here the primary concept of organ prevails.

Corresponding to the concept of organ in the narrower sense of an official functionary is a particular and narrower concept of the state *qua* aggregate of official organs. This frequently used concept is also expressed in the somewhat naive notion that the state is a narrower, more fixed organization within a state in the broader sense, which comprises all citizens. The concept of the state as organ—organ *qua* person—is indeed graphic, because it is personifying; but that does not make it correct, and from the standpoint of an exact structural analysis, it must be replaced by the concept of the state as organ *qua* function. One of the elements making up the material fact of the organ *qua* function is, to be sure, the specific qualification of the human being performing the function, the so-called organ- or function-bearer personified in the concept of state organ. But if one replaces state organ with state function, then the state—which one speaks of as the aggregate of official state organs, the bureaucracy—shows itself to be a system of legally particular functions. These are, namely, those functions that are to be performed by individuals qualified in a specific way as state officials by the legal system; in addition to these, there are other functions, like legislation, that are performed by organs not specifically qualified as officials. This state is an aggregate of material facts legally qualified in a specific way, and so, ultimately, it is a system comprising the legal norms that qualify these material facts. It is a legal system *qua* subsystem, more or less arbitrarily singled out from the state legal system as a whole.

(d) Political Theory as Legal Theory

That the state is a legal system is corroborated by the fact that problems traditionally depicted from the standpoint of a general political theory prove to be problems in legal theory, problems of the validity and creation of the legal system. What one calls 'elements' of the state—state power, state territory, and the citizenry—are simply the validity of the state system *per se*, along with the territorial and personal spheres of validity of the system. A special case within the general question of the territorial sphere of validity of the norms forming the state system is the question of the nature of those legal structures that emerge when the territory of the state is subdivided. These are problems of centralization and decentralization, and from this standpoint one is able to comprehend administrative decentralization, self-administering bodies, member states of a federal system, state fragments, and so on—but also, in particular, all coalitions of states. The doctrine of the threefold powers or functions of the state proves to be focused on the legal system's various hierarchical levels of creation; organs of the state can be understood only as material facts of law creation and application, and the forms of state are nothing but methods of creating the legal system, which one regards, figuratively speaking, as the 'will of the state'.

(e) Power of the State as Efficacy of the Legal System

Just as one recognizes in the coercive legal system the state *qua* system, and one recognizes in the personification of this system's unity the state *qua* person, so one can comprehend in the efficacy of the legal system the state *qua* 'power'—everything that one traditionally characterizes as the 'power of the state'. This power can express itself only in the motivating force of the notions contained in the norms of the legal system, that is, the state system. All of the external displays in which one traditionally perceives the power of the state—the prisons and fortresses, the gallows and machine guns—all of these are in and of themselves lifeless objects. They become tools of state power only in so far as human beings make use of them in accordance with a certain system, only in so far as these human beings are governed by the notion of this system, by the belief that they ought to act in conformity with this system.

Taking all this into account, one sees that the dualism of law and state is resolved as the familiar mistake[71] of doubling the object of cognition, which occurs when the cognizing theorist, having established the unity of the object of cognition and expressed it in the concept of person, goes on to hypostatize that unity, to posit the person as real, concrete. And then the dualism of state *qua* person and law *qua* legal system, considered from an epistemological standpoint, is parallel to the similarly contradictory dualism of God and the world. Political ideology in public law, essentially in agreement with theologico-religious ideology, appears merely as an offshoot of the latter and a substitute for it. If, however, one recognizes the identity of law and state, then it is impossible to justify the state by way of the law. For if one comprehends that the law—positive law, not to be identified with justice—is exactly the same coercive system as the state shows itself to be when cognition dispels anthropomorphic pictures and cuts through the veil of personification to the real connections between human beings, then one can no more justify the state by way of the law than one can justify the law by way of the law—unless 'law' is used one time in the sense of positive law, the other time in the sense of 'right' law, of justice. The attempt to legitimize the state as a *Rechtsstaat* is exposed as completely inappropriate, since every state must be a *Rechtsstaat* —if one understands by '*Rechtsstaat*' a state that 'has' a legal system. There can be no state that does not have, or does not yet have, a legal system, since every state is only a legal system (this is not a political value-judgment of any kind). Of course, one must not confuse this concept of the *Rechtsstaat* with the concept of a legal system having a particular content, namely, a legal system comprising certain institutions, such as individual liberties, guarantees of legality in the functioning of organs, and democratic methods of creating law. To perceive a 'true' legal system only in a system of norms fashioned along these lines is a prejudice of natural law. From the standpoint of a logically consistent legal positivism, the law, exactly like the state, cannot be comprehended as anything other than a coercive system of human behaviour—which is to say nothing about that system's

[71] See esp. §§ 25, 48(*b*) (the last sentence).

values of morality or justice. The state, then, is to be understood in legal terms, no more and no less so than the law itself; the law *qua* ideal subject-matter[72] is a system, and therefore an object of normative-legal cognition, while the law *qua* act—both motivated and motivating, both psychological and physical—is power, legal power, and as such an object of enquiry for social psychology or sociology.

(f) Resolving the Ideology of Legitimacy

Resolving the dualism of law and state by way of this methodological critique amounts to the uncompromising destruction of one of the most effective ideologies of legitimacy, prompting traditional legal and political theory to resist with a vengeance the thesis established by the Pure Theory, namely, the identity of law and state.

When the Pure Theory of Law rejects a legitimization of the state by way of the law, it does so not because, say, it declares every legitimization of the state to be impossible. The Pure Theory denies only that legal science has the capacity to justify the state by way of the law, or, what comes to the same thing, to justify the law by way of the state. The Pure Theory denies in particular that it can be the task of legal science to justify anything whatever. Justification means evaluation, which is always subjective and therefore a matter of ethics and politics, not of objective cognition. It is objective cognition alone that legal science, too, must serve, if it aims to be a science and not politics.

[72] 'ideal subject-matter' ('*geistiger Sachgehalt*'). On '*Geist*', see § 8, n. 12, above, and Supplementary Note 3, in appendix I.

IX

The State and International Law

§ 49. The Nature of International Law

(a) Hierarchical Levels of International Law; its Basic Norm

International law consists of norms that were created to regulate interstate relations, norms originally created by way of acts of states, that is, the acts of organs duly authorized by the legal systems of the individual states. These are norms originally created by way of custom. They are the norms of general international law because they impose obligations on, and grant rights to, all states. Among them, the norm known as *pacta sunt servanda* is of special significance. It empowers the subjects of the international legal community [namely, the individual states] to govern their behaviour by means of treaties—that is, the behaviour of their organs and citizens. The process consists in creating norms by way of the declared agreement of duly authorized organs of two or more states, norms that impose obligations on, and grant rights to, the states entering into the treaty. Treaty law in force today has simply the character of particular international law. Its norms are valid not for all states but only for a given pair of states, or for a group of states, sometimes larger, sometimes smaller. These paired states and groups of states constitute subcommunities of the international legal community. It should be noted here that particular international treaty law and general international customary law are not to be regarded as coordinated groups of norms. Since the basis of particular international treaty law is a norm belonging to the group of norms of general international customary law, the relation between the two is a relation between lower and higher hierarchical levels. And if one also considers the legal norms created by way of international courts and similar organs, then yet a third level is apparent in the structure of international law, for the function of such organs, which create international law, is itself based on a treaty, and thus on a norm of the second hierarchical level of international law. This second level—international law created by way of international treaties—is based in turn on a principle of general international customary law, the first or highest of the hierarchical strata. The basic norm of international law, then, and thus of state legal systems, too, whose powers are delegated to them by international law, must be a norm that establishes custom—the reciprocal behaviour of the states—as a law-creating material fact. Although general international customary law is more recent in origin than the state legal systems, this does not stand in the way of its serving as the basis of their validity. The family, too, is an older legal community than the centralized state, which encompasses many families; yet the state legal system presently serves as the basis of the validity of family law. Similarly for a federation: the validity of a member state's system derives from the constitution of the federation, even though the system antedates the federation of once independent individual states. One must not confuse historical sequence with the logical relation between norms.

(b) International Law as Primitive Legal System

International law exhibits the same character as the law of individual states. Like the latter, it is a coercive system. And in the reconstructed legal norm of international law, as in the reconstructed legal norm of the state legal system, a material fact (regarded as harmful to the community) is linked with a coercive act, as condition with consequence. In international law, the specific consequences of an unlawful act are reprisal and war. International law is still a primitive legal system, however, just at the beginning of a development that the state legal system has already completed. It is still marked by wide-ranging decentralization—at least in the field of general international law, and thus as it affects the entire international legal community. There are still no organs, whose respective functions reflect a division of labour, for creating and applying legal norms. The formation of general norms proceeds by way of custom or treaty, which is to say, by way of the members of the legal community themselves, and not by way of a special legislative organ. And the application of general norms to the concrete case proceeds in the same way. The state that considers its interests violated is to decide for itself whether there exists the material fact of an unlawful act for which another state is responsible. And if this other state denies the claimed unlawful act, then, for want of an objective authority to settle the dispute in a legally regulated procedure, the state whose law has been violated is itself authorized to respond to the violator with a coercive act of general international law, that is, with reprisal or war. This self-help technique, which also served as the point of departure for the development of the state legal system, emphasizes the principles of collective and absolute liability over the principles of individual liability and liability for fault. The consequence of an unlawful act is not directed against the human being who, functioning as an organ of the individual state, intentionally or negligently brought about the material fact of the unlawful act. Rather, the consequence is directed against others, who took no part in the unlawful act and were unable to prevent it. Reprisals and war do not strike the state organs whose acts or for-bearances, imputed to the state, count as violations of international law; reprisals and war strike either the mass of human beings making up 'the people', or they strike a particular state organ, the army—in so far as it is possible, in modern warfare, to separate the army from the people at all.

(c) Indirectly Imposing Obligations and Granting Rights by way of International Law

International law imposes obligations on, and grants rights to, states. It is incorrect to assume—as is usually done—that this means that international law does not impose obligations on, and grant rights to, individual human beings. Since all law is essentially the governing of human behaviour, the content of a legal obligation as well as that of a legal right can only be human behaviour (other material facts are included only in so far as they are connected with human behaviour); and human behaviour can only be the behaviour of individual human beings. To say that international law imposes obligations on, and grants rights to, states means simply that it imposes obligations on, and grants rights to, individual human beings indirectly, mediated by the directly governing state legal system (for which 'state', after all, is simply the personifying expression). Imposing obligations on, and granting rights to, a state by way of international law has the same character as imposing obligations on, and granting rights to, a legal person by way of the state legal system. The state is a legal person, and the norms of international law, which impose obligations on, and grant rights to, states *qua* legal persons, are incomplete, requiring completion. They determine only the objective element, not the subjective element, of the human behaviour that is necessarily their content. They determine only what ought to be done or forborne, and not who— which individual human being—is to do or to forbear from doing. International law leaves the determination of this individual to the state legal system. This delegation to the state fully captures the legal sense of that property of international law according to which 'international law imposes obligations on, and grants rights to, states alone', or 'states alone are subjects of international law'. What is expressed thereby is simply that international law imposes obligations on, and grants rights to, individual human beings indirectly, mediated by the state legal system.

While international law, as a rule, comprehends individual human behaviour only indirectly, there are significant exceptions to this in the fields of both general international customary law and particular international treaty law. There are cases where international law imposes obligations on, and grants rights to, individual human beings directly, in that a norm of international law determines not only what ought to be done or forborne, but also—directly—which individual human being is to do or to forbear from doing. These are cases, then, where individual human beings are directly subjects of international law. To the same extent that its governing reaches to matters previously regulated by the state legal system alone, international law must grow in its tendency to impose obligations on, and grant rights to, individuals directly. At the same time and to the same extent, individual liability and liability for fault must replace collective and absolute liability. Hand in hand with this goes a development that can presently be observed only within particular international legal communities, namely, the development of

central organs for creating and applying legal norms. This
centralization, exactly as in the evolution of the state legal
system, begins with adjudication; its aim is the development of
an international jurisdiction.

§ 50. The Unity of International Law and State Law

(a) The Unity of the Object of Enquiry: An Epistemological Postulate

Evolution in terms of legal technique, alluded to here, tends in
the end to blur the distinction between international law and the
state legal system. The result is that actual development of the
law, directed as it is to increasing centralization, appears to have
as its ultimate goal the organizational unity of a universal legal
community—that is, the development of a world state. At the
present time, however, there can be no talk of a world state. The
only given is a cognitive unity of all law; that is, one can conceive
of international law together with the state legal systems as a
unified system of norms in exactly the same way as one is
accustomed to regarding the state legal system as a unity.

The notion of the cognitive unity of all law is in conflict with
the tradition, which is inclined to see international law and state
law as two different systems of norms, independent of each other
and reciprocally isolated because resting on two different basic
norms. But this dualistic construction—better characterized as
'pluralistic', considering the multiplicity of state legal systems—
is not tenable even on purely logical grounds if the norms of
international law as well as those of the state legal systems are to
be viewed as simultaneously valid norms, and indeed, if the norms
of both alike are to be viewed as legal norms. This view, shared
even by proponents of the dualistic doctrine, reflects the epistemological requirement that all law be considered in one system,
that it be considered from one and the same standpoint as an
integral whole in itself. Because legal cognition aims to comprehend as law—to comprehend within the category of the valid
legal norm—material characterized as international law, as well as
material presenting itself as state law, legal cognition sets the very
same task for itself that natural science sets for itself: to represent

its object as a unity. The negative criterion of this unity is non-contradiction, a logical principle that also applies to cognition in the realm of norms. One cannot claim that a norm with content A is valid, and claim at the same time that a norm with content not-A is valid. One can claim—and no doubt must claim, in view of the facts—that norms whose content is mutually exclusive actually are issued and, on the part of the norm-addressees, are imagined and are obeyed or not obeyed. There is no more a logical contradiction in this statement, referring to natural facts, than there is in the observation that two opposing forces are both efficacious. But one cannot claim that two norms whose content is, logically speaking, mutually exclusive are valid at the same time— that is, one cannot claim that A ought to be and, at the same time, not-A ought to be, just as one cannot claim that A is and, at the same time, not-A is. If legal cognition encounters legal norms that contradict one another in content, it seeks, by interpreting their meaning, to resolve the contradiction as a mere pseudo-contradiction. If this effort fails, legal cognition disposes of the material to be interpreted, disposes of it as lacking in meaning altogether and therefore as non-existent in the legal sphere *qua* realm of meaning. What is established thereby is simply a predisposition inherent in legal cognition, [a predisposition in favour of unity]. This process was depicted earlier, in the context of the problem of interpretation.[73]

(b) Reciprocal Relation between Two Systems of Norms

Since the jurist regards international law, like the state legal system, as a complex of valid or binding norms, and not—or not merely—as a conglomerate of natural facts, he must conceive of these complexes of norms in one non-contradictory system. There are, in principle, two possibilities for a unified system. Two complexes of norms, apparently different, form a unified system if one complex (or system) proves to be subordinate to the other because the basis of its validity—and so, its (relative) basic norm, the basic determinant of its creation—is found in the other system, that is, in a norm of the other system. Or, alternatively, the two systems appear as coordinates of one another, equally ordered, which really means that they are

[73] See §§ 31(h), 35–7.

separated from each other in their spheres of validity. Coordinate systems presuppose a third, higher-order system that governs the creation of both of the other systems, separating them from each other in their spheres of validity, and thus, first and foremost, coordinating them. It is clear from what has been said in earlier contexts[74] that the determination of the sphere of validity is the determination of an element of the content of the lower-level norm by the higher-level norm. The process of [norm] creation can be determined directly or indirectly, depending on whether the higher-level norm itself determines the process whereby the lower-level norm is created, or whether the higher-level norm confines itself to establishing an authority that is empowered to use its own discretion to create norms that are valid for a certain area. Here one speaks of delegation; and the unity comprising the linked higher- and lower-order systems has the character of a chain of delegation. It follows, then, that the higher-order system, which delegates powers to various lower-order systems, must bear the same relation to those systems as that of a comprehensive system to its subsystems; that is to say, since the (relative) basic norm of the lower-order system is a component of the higher-order system, the lower-order system can be thought of as being contained in the higher-order system *qua* comprehensive system. The basic norm of the higher-order system, as the highest hierarchical level of the collective system, represents the ultimate basis of validity of all norms, including the norms of the lower-order systems.

If international law and state law form a unified system, then their reciprocal relation must take shape in one of these two ways.

(c) Monistic or Dualistic Construction

A monistic construction—which, from the standpoint of the Pure Theory of Law, is simply an epistemological corollary—is confronted with the particular objection that the possibility of irresolvable contradictions between the content of international law and that of the state legal system results in the reciprocal independence of the two. If this claim were correct, one plainly could not make the claim that the state legal system and

[74] See §§ 6, 31(a)–(b).

international law are both valid systems of norms, or even that
two state legal systems are both valid. For one cannot claim the
simultaneous validity of two independent, possibly contradictory legal systems, any more than one can assume the simultaneous validity of morality and the positive law, which is in fact
entirely independent of morality. If morality contradicts the
positive law, then the jurist, operating with provisions of the
positive law as valid norms, must leave morality out of
consideration. So, too, the dualistic construction would have to
confine itself to regarding the legal system of a single state—of
one's own state, say, a system whose unity is presupposed as self-
evident—as the only system of valid legal norms. Other state
legal systems and, in particular, international law—more
precisely, the material so characterized—would have to be
considered, then, not as falling within the category of the valid
norm, and therefore not as law proper, that is, not in terms of
their normativity (which marks the legal system of one's own
state first and foremost as law), but simply in terms of their
facticity. This is the standpoint of primitive man, who, with
utmost presumption, acknowledges as a legal community only
his own community, and as a legal system only the system
constituting his own community. Accordingly, he considers all
those not belonging to his community as lawless 'barbarians',
and if he considers their system as a system at all, it is certainly
not as true 'law', comparable in kind and in value to his own
law. In this view, there can be no genuine international law
either.

It is a view that has not been fully overcome even today. It
lives on, to a certain degree, in the notion that only the system of
one's own state is 'law', law proper in the full sense of the word.
And this is the point of departure taken, for the most part
unwittingly, by the dualistic theory.

(d) Primacy of the State Legal System

In practice, it is next to impossible to deny straightaway the
normative character not only of international law but also of
state systems other than one's own, so the dualistic construction
must resort to a fiction in order to account for the legal nature of
complexes of norms outside the legal system of one's own state.

It is, namely, the doctrine that if international law is to be binding for one's own state, and if states other than one's own are to be considered as legal communities vis-à-vis one's own state, then they must be 'recognized' as such by one's own state. In this way, the basis for the validity of both international law and state legal systems other than one's own is built into the legal system of one's own state, into the 'will' of one's own state *qua* highest legal entity in the social sphere. International law, valid only if a state recognizes it as binding for that state, does not appear, then, either as a supra-state legal system or as a legal system independent of, and isolated from, the system of one's own state; rather, in so far as international law appears as law at all, it is as a freely incorporated component of the legal system of one's own state, as 'external state law', that is, as the aggregate of those norms of the state legal system that govern behaviour toward other states, and that are adopted by way of 'recognition'. Since the legal existence of other states also rests on recognition by one's own state, the legal system of one's own state must be imagined as extending over the legal systems of the other states. It is as though the legal system of one's own state, having adopted international law, were to delegate powers to the other states, that is, to the appropriate law-creating authorities for those territories. This is the theoretical sense of the doctrine that other states must be recognized by one's own state in order to qualify as states, that is, as valid legal systems, seen from the standpoint of one's own state, too, as binding for their territories. The doctrine of recognition establishes a chain of delegation that links a state legal system—the system serving as the point of departure for the construction—to all other state legal systems. But with that, the predisposition inherent in legal cognition prevails—even against the will of the predisposed—and once again the unity of the legal world-view is established. Not on the basis of the primacy of the international legal system, to be sure, but on the basis of the primacy of the state legal system.

The necessity of comprehending as valid legal norms not only the legal system of one's own state, but also other state legal systems and, in particular, international law, drives the dualistic construction to self-destruct on the doctrine of recognition indispensable to it. And the consequences of the dualistic construction, never entirely worked out by its own proponents, exhibit clearly the political design underlying the dualistic view, namely, the interest in preserving the notion of the sovereignty of the state, the notion that the state represents, in absolute terms, the highest legal community. This sovereignty, of course, can only be that of one's own state, which serves as the point of departure for the entire dualistic construction; for the sovereignty of one state—'sovereignty' in its original, absolute sense—is incompatible with the sovereignty of another state.

The dogma of state sovereignty, resulting in the primacy of the legal system of one's own state, corresponds completely to a subjectivistic view that ultimately collapses into solipsism, the view that would comprehend the single individual, the 'I', as the centre of the world, and the world, therefore, merely as something willed and imagined by the 'I'. This is a radical state-subjectivism, confronted by a specifically objectivistic view of the world and the law, the view that finds expression in the primacy of the international legal system.

(e) Denying International Law

The subjectivist's own 'I' is his point of departure in comprehending the world, but despite extending it to the universe, the subjectivist cannot get past his own sovereign 'I' to arrive at an objective world. He is incapable of comprehending another subject, the not-'I', as an entity comparable to his own 'I', with the same claim to sovereignty, the 'you' also aiming to be an 'I'. Similarly, a monistic construction based on the primacy of the legal system of one's own state is completely incompatible with the notion of a plurality of coordinate states, equally ordered and legally separated from each other in their spheres of validity. (And it is precisely this monistic construction that dualism, with its bias for preserving the dogma of sovereignty, transforms itself into by way of the doctrine of recognition.) Thus, the primacy of the state legal system implies in the end not only the denial of the sovereignty of all other states, and thereby their legal existence as states (in terms of the dogma of sovereignty), but also the denial of international law.

That is to say, international law is forced to undergo a complete denaturing in the notion that it is incorporated into the legal system of one's own state. For within the confines of a state legal system, international law can no longer perform its essential function of coordinating, of equally ordering, all states. The basis for the validity of the norms governing the behaviour of one's own state toward other states—the validity, that is, of international law *qua* external state law—lies in the constitution of the state adopting international law. The validity of international law can be abrogated, then, according to the rules of this constitution—in the most extreme case, by way of a constitutional amendment. Also abrogated thereby, however, would be the recognition of other states—dependent as it is on the provisions of [international law *qua*] external state law—and thus the legal nature of the systems of those states, solely dependent as it is, in turn, on such recognition. The theory of the primacy of the legal system of one's own state returns ultimately to its point of departure, namely, that one acknowledge as law only the legal system of one's own state.

Given the ideological nature of the law, characterizing the meaning of certain material facts as law is the result (as shown earlier)[75] not of a necessary interpretation, but simply of a possible interpretation, requiring the presupposition of the basic norm. One cannot deny, therefore, the theoretical possibility of the position that what is interpreted as law is only the system of one's own state, including whatever can be comprehended as deriving from that system. However, if one believes that the consequences stemming from the primacy of the legal system of one's own state should be avoided, then the notion of the primacy of the international legal system is indispensable.

(f) Resolving the 'Contradiction' between International Law and State Law

The fiction necessarily employed in the dualistic construction is that if international law is to be valid for the individual state, it must be recognized by that state. And in this very fiction lies the answer to the principal objection raised against a monistic construction of the relation between international law and state law: the objection, namely, that irresolvable contradictions are possible between the two. For how can there be these irresolvable contradictions if it is the same 'will' that both recognizes

[75] See § 16.

international law and represents itself as the state legal system? And the possibility of such contradictions seems all the more dubious when one considers that this so-called 'will' of the state is simply the anthropomorphic expression for the 'ought' of norms. Moreover, that which is characterized as a 'contradiction' between international law and state law has nothing to do with logical contradiction; rather, it is simply a special case of the aforementioned conflict between a higher-level norm and a lower-level norm.[76] That which one claims to be a 'contradiction' between international law and state law—the fact, say, that a state statute is in opposition to a treaty that the state has entered into with another state—would not affect the validity of either the state norm or the norm of international law, just as, within the state legal system, completely analogous instances would not call the unity of the system into question. Even the unconstitutional statute is, and remains, a valid statute, without the constitution necessarily being regarded as repealed or amended because of it. Even the judicial decision contrary to statute is a valid norm, and remains valid until it is overturned by another judicial decision. As shown in an earlier context,[77] the 'norm contrariety' of a norm does not amount to a logical contradiction between the lower-level norm and the higher-level norm; rather, it simply represents either the invalidatability of the lower-level norm, or the responsible authority's liability to punishment. In this connection, it should be noted that the issuance of a norm 'contrary to norm' may be the material fact of an unlawful act to which the legal system attaches its specific coercive acts as consequence. It is clear from what has been said earlier[78] that even the material fact of an unlawful act as such does not logically contradict the norm that establishes it as an unlawful act. There is no logical difficulty, then, in creating valid legal norms by way of an act that is qualified as an illegality. The consequences of an unlawful act may be attached to the issuance of a norm, but the norm thus issued may be none the less valid—not simply in the sense that it remains valid until it is overturned by way of a legal act [in a prescribed procedure], but even in the sense that [lacking such a procedure] it cannot be overturned at all on the basis of the claim of its deficiency.

[76] See § 31(h).   [77] See § 31(h).
[78] See § 14(b).

The latter is the case in the relation between international law and state law. That international law obligates the state to perform certain acts, and, in particular, to issue norms of a certain content, means simply that a contrary act, or the issuance of a state norm of contrary content, is the condition to which international law attaches its specific sanction—reprisal or war—as the consequence of an unlawful act. Norms of the state legal system that are created by 'violating' international law remain valid, even from the standpoint of international law, because international law makes no provision for a procedure whereby norms of the state legal system that are 'contrary to international law' can be invalidated. Such a possibility exists only in the field of particular international law. The relation of international law to norms of the state legal system that are called 'contrary to international law' is the same, then, as the relation of a state constitution that determines the content of future statutes—say, in its catalogue of civil rights—to statutes that violate civil rights and are therefore unconstitutional. That is, the relation is the same given that the constitution—as is usually the case—does not establish a procedure for overturning statutes on the basis of their unconstitutionality, that it confines itself instead to the possibility of holding certain authorities personally responsible for enacting the so-called unconstitutional statute. The content of the state legal system is determined by international law in exactly the same way as the content of future statutes is determined by a constitution lacking provision for constitutional review, that is, content is determined in terms of alternatives. The possibility of content other than the prescribed content is not precluded, and precisely because this other content is not precluded, it is authorized, even if only as a secondary alternative. Its disqualification lies simply in the fact that the issuance of such norms is qualified—without prejudice to their validity—as the material fact of an unlawful act. Neither this unlawful act nor the norm created thereby, characterized as 'contrary to international law', logically contradicts international law. From this vantage-point, then, nothing stands in the way of assuming the unity of international law and state law.

(g) Primacy of the International Legal System

Unity, thus understood, is preserved not only negatively, in the absence of logical contradiction between the two complexes of norms, but also positively, in the assumption—quite generally made, especially by proponents of the dualistic construction— that the states or, expressed without personification, the state legal systems are mutually coordinated and legally separated from each other in their spheres of validity, in particular, their territorial spheres. This assumption is possible only if one presupposes, above the state legal systems, a legal system coordinating them and separating them from each other in their spheres of validity, a legal system that can only be—and, indeed, is—the international legal system. For these are the functions performed by the norms of positive international law.

As mentioned earlier,[79] it is a principle of general international law, recognized in both theory and practice, that (in the familiar wording) even a government that comes to power by revolutionary means or a *coup d'état* is to be regarded, in terms of international law, as legitimate if it is capable of securing continuous obedience to the norms it issues. What this really means is that a coercive system directly under international law is to be regarded, in terms of international law, as a legitimate, binding legal system—or, in other words, that the community constituted by such a system is to be regarded as a state—for precisely that area where reality corresponds, by and large, to the system. When this principle of effectiveness, this basic principle of positive international law, is applied to state legal systems, it amounts to their authorization by international law. If establishing a norm-issuing power whose system is continuously effective for a certain area represents, in terms of positive law, the emergence of a lawmaking authority, it is because international law invests the authority with this property, which means that international law empowers the authority to make law. But with that, international law also determines the spatial and temporal sphere of validity of the state legal system formed thereby. The territory of the individual state, which is the spatial sphere of validity of the state legal system, extends—because of international law—as far as the legal system is effective. And

[79] See § 30(c).

international law guarantees this territorial sphere of validity by attaching its specific consequence (reprisal or war) to the unlawful act of an intrusion into the area under its protection. Separating the state legal systems from each other in their spheres of validity consists essentially—apart from certain exceptions—in permitting each state, on principle, to appear in its capacity as a coercive apparatus only within its own territory, that is, the territory guaranteed to it by international law. Or, speaking non-figuratively, such separation consists in the fact that the state legal system is to establish its own specific coercive acts only for the spatial sphere of validity granted to it by international law, and that only within this space can these coercive acts be brought about without violating international law. In this way, the spatial juxtaposition of a plurality of states, that is, the juxtaposition of a plurality of coercive systems, becomes legally possible. But international law determines not only juxtaposition in space, it also determines succession in time, that is, the temporal sphere of validity of the state legal systems. The beginning and end of the legal validity of a state system are dependent on the legal principle of effectiveness. Seen from this standpoint, the rise and fall of the state—like the establishment and dissolution of a legal person in the framework of intra-state law—show themselves to be legal phenomena. And even with regard to the material sphere of validity of the state legal systems, international law is significant. Since its norms, in particular those created by treaty, can embrace all possible objects, and thus even those objects previously regulated by the state legal systems, international law limits the material sphere of validity of those systems. To be sure, the individual states remain—under international law, too—competent in principle to regulate everything, but they retain this competence only in so far as international law does not appropriate for itself an object to regulate, thus withdrawing the object from unconstrained regulation by the state legal system. If, then, one presupposes international law as a supra-state legal system, the state legal system no longer has absolute sovereignty. It does have a claim to totality, however, subject only to the constraints of international law; that is to say, the state legal system is not limited at the outset by international law to [the regulation of] certain objects, which is the case with other legal systems or communities directly under international law, namely, those legal systems and communities constituted by treaty.

(h) State as Organ of the International Legal Community

The concept of the state can now be characterized using the international legal system as the point of departure. The state, then, is a relatively centralized legal system *qua* subsystem, directly under international law. Its territorial and temporal sphere of validity is limited by international law, and with regard to its material sphere of validity, it has a claim to totality subject only to the constraints of international law.

In the familiar personification, this legal system *qua* subsystem—the individual state—can be characterized as an organ of the international legal community. It is only as such that the individual state participates in creating international law. This insight is of particular significance for the creation of international law by way of treaty, which, in the view of many writers, is the only way that prevailing international law can be changed and further developed. Accordingly, they fictionalize as a tacit treaty the creation of law by way of custom, which gives rise primarily to general international law; and they do so simply to maintain the dogma of sovereignty, simply to be able to trace the validity of international law back to the free will of the individual state. This construction, however, rests on a self-deception. If the treaty is regarded as a law-creating material fact, then the norm created by treaty imposes obligations on, and grants rights to, not just one but both of the states entering into the treaty and mutually coordinated thereby, which really means that the norm imposes obligations on, and grants rights to, the organs and citizens of both states, albeit only indirectly. If this is to be the case, then a norm must be presupposed that establishes the state treaty as a law-creating material fact. And this presupposed norm cannot be a norm of the state legal system; it can only be a component of a higher-order legal system, above the state legal systems and, first and foremost, coordinating them. For a norm of the state legal system—or, figuratively speaking, the will of the individual state—cannot impose obligations on, and grant rights to, another state, that is, the organs and citizens of another state. If states are coordinates of one another, equally ordered, then each state can impose obligations on, and grant rights to, only its own citizens. The competence of a state does not reach beyond the sphere of validity of the state legal system. And since the competence of one state and that of another cannot be added up like mathematical quantities, then—unless a higher-order system delegates appropriate powers—not even two states together are in a position to create norms that, like norms created by state treaty, are valid for the territory of both states. The creation of norms of international law can be theoretically comprehended only from the standpoint of general international law, which governs such law creation by qualifying the state treaty in particular as a law-creating method, that is, by obligating the states to act in accordance with treaty. From this standpoint, the state representatives who are active in concluding a treaty between their two states make up a compound but unitary organ, an organ of the community of states constituted by general international law, and not, say, a common organ of both states. Power is delegated by international law to the state legal system to determine which individual is to express, in the name of the state, the state's will vis-à-vis the treaty; and therefore the state representatives active in concluding the treaty are, as suborgans of the collective organ creating the treaty norm, primarily organs of the international legal community. Each of these suborgans is only secondarily an organ of its own state. Thus, it is not really individual states that create international law by way of treaty, as those writers influenced by the dogma of sovereignty usually stress; rather, it is the community of states or, more correctly, the international legal community—just as it is the state that creates state law by way of state organs.

The state *qua* organ of international law is simply a metaphor, standing for the state legal system that is linked to the international legal system and, mediated by the latter, to all other state legal systems, forging the chain of delegation whose structure was outlined above.[80]

This chain of delegation establishes, in a thoroughly positive-law sense, the unity of the universal legal system. To avoid misunderstandings, one must emphasize vigorously and repeatedly that this unity is simply cognitive, not organizational.

[80] See § 50(b),(d).

Within its fabric, the individual state *qua* legal entity is freed of the ossifying absolutism of the dogma of sovereignty. The Pure Theory of Law relativizes the state. And by recognizing the state as an intermediate level of the law, the Pure Theory discerns that a continuous sequence of legal structures, gradually merging into one another, leads from the universal legal community of international law, encompassing all states, to the legal communities incorporated into the state.

(i) Pure Theory of Law and Development of World Law

The theoretical dissolution of the dogma of sovereignty, the principal instrument of imperialistic ideology directed against international law, is one of the most substantial achievements of the Pure Theory of Law. Although it was certainly not arrived at by political design, it is an achievement that may nevertheless have political import. For it eliminates a nearly insurmountable barrier confronting every technical improvement in international law, every effort toward further centralization of the international legal system. The Pure Theory of Law opposes a line of argumentation that pronounces such development incompatible with the nature of international law or with the essence of the state—which is really to say, incompatible with all that the concept of sovereignty is supposed to express. The Pure Theory of Law exposes once and for all the attempt to use the concept of sovereignty to lend to a purely political argument—which is always vulnerable to a comparable counter-argument—the appearance of a logical argument, which would by its very nature be irrefutable. And precisely by exposing the argument as political, the Pure Theory of Law facilitates development that has been stunted by mistaken notions, development in terms of legal policy—facilitates such development, but does not justify or postulate it. For that is a matter of complete indifference to the Pure Theory of Law *qua* theory.

To point out the possibility of political import cannot besmirch the purity of the Pure Theory. Even the exact natural sciences, which alone make technical progress possible, do so without intending it—indeed, do so precisely because nothing but pure cognition is their aim. With this in mind, it may be said that the Pure Theory of Law, because it secures the cognitive unity of all law by relativizing the concept of the state, creates a presupposition not without significance for the organizational unity of a centralized system of world law.

Appendix I

Supplementary Notes

These supplementary notes follow up on a few of the brief footnotes that we have added to the text proper.

1. 'Legal science' ('*Rechtswissenschaft*'), § 1, n. 1. Kelsen's statement that the Pure Theory of Law is *legal science* suggests the ambiguity of the term 'legal science' in his writings. He often uses the term to mean academic enquiry into positive law, but here, by saying that 'legal science' also includes within its scope the Pure Theory of Law, he expands the term to include enquiry into general theoretical assumptions underlying the law. On this broader reading, legal science properly comprises legal theory; on the narrower view, it does not.

For a helpful discussion on the different readings of 'legal science' in Kelsen's work generally, see J. W. Harris, 'Kelsen and Normative Consistency', in *Essays on Kelsen*, ed. Richard Tur and William Twining (Oxford: Clarendon Press, 1986), 201–28, at 203–5. For a general discussion on the language of legal science in the work of contemporary legal theorists, see Richard E. Susskind, *Expert Systems in Law. A Jurisprudential Inquiry* (Oxford: Clarendon Press, 1987), at 75–80. A number of writers offer perspectives on legal science; see e.g. Anders Wedberg, 'Some Problems in the Logical Analysis of Legal Science', *Theoria*, 17 (1951), 246–75, repr. (with minor changes) in *Contemporary Philosophy in Scandinavia*, ed. Raymond E. Wilson and Anthony M. Paul (Baltimore: Johns Hopkins Press, 1972), 237–56; R. H. S. Tur, 'The Notion of a Legal Right: A Test Case for Legal Science', *Juridical Review*, 21 (1976), 177–88; J. W. Harris, *Law and Legal Science* (Oxford: Clarendon Press, 1979); N. E. Simmonds, *The Decline of Juridical Reason* (Manchester: Manchester UP, 1984), at 1–36, 82–98; Vittorio Villa, 'Legal Science between Natural and Human Sciences', *Legal Studies*, 4 (1984), 243–70; and Peter Goodrich, *Legal Discourse* (New York:

St Martin's Press, 1987), at 32–44. See also the perspective of the distinguished legal theorist and legal historian Hermann U. Kantorowicz, in 'Legal Science—A Survey of its Methodology', *Columbia Law Review*, 28 (1928), 679–707 (notes by Edwin W. Patterson), and in Kantorowicz, *The Definition of Law*, ed. A. H. Campbell, intro. by A. L. Goodhart (Cambridge: Cambridge UP, 1958).

The older expression for 'legal science', from the days when German legal instruction was offered in Latin, is *'Jurisprudenz'* (Lat. *'iurisprudentia'*). It is still used occasionally (see Kelsen's own use in § 1, text at n. 3), sometimes to emphasize technical legal skill and know-how, which are ill served by *'Rechtswissenschaft'*, with its severe 'scientific' connotations.

The distinction Kelsen makes between the terms 'legal dogmatics' and 'general legal theory' is comparable, in part, to that between his narrower and his broader reading of 'legal science', above. In an article appearing a few years after the present work, he writes:

> One may represent systematically a particular legal system, e.g., the law of France or international law; or one may emphasize a certain group of norms of a particular legal system, e.g., Swedish criminal law or the German law of contracts; or one may emphasize an individual legal rule, e.g., the Swiss Civil Code regulation of interest for default. In all these cases, one is concerned with legal dogmatics (*Rechtsdogmatik*). . . [which may be] linked with legal interpretation.

Kelsen sketches two other approaches to legal cognition, namely, legal history and comparative law, and continues:

> Finally, one may also . . . enquire into the very nature of the law, its typical structure apart from its changing content at different times and in different places. This is the task of general legal theory (*allgemeine Rechtslehre*), i.e., legal theory that is not restricted to a particular legal system or to particular legal norms. General legal theory . . . provides the theoretical basis for all other branches of legal science.

And he adds:

> The Pure Theory of Law is neither the dogmatics nor the interpretation of a particular legal system, nor is it legal history or comparative law. Rather, it is general legal theory.

Kelsen, 'The Function of the Pure Theory of Law', in *Law. A Century of Progress 1835–1935*, vol. ii (New York: New York UP,

1937), 231–41, at 231–2. (The passage quoted is our own translation from the original, German-language text: 'Die Ziele der Reinen Rechtslehre', published in 1936 in Bratislava.)

In passing, a word on our translation of '*rechtswissenschaftliche*' in the title of the present work. Kelsen's entirely theoretical focus in the work, along with his preference for the term 'theory' ('*Lehre*') rather than 'science' ('*Wissenschaft*') in the name he gives to his own Pure Theory of Law, coupled lastly with the connotations of 'dogmatics' that stem from the narrower reading of 'legal science' and are inappropriate here—all argue in favour of translating Kelsen's subtitle,'*Einleitung in die rechtswissenschaftliche Problematik*', as 'Introduction to the Problems of Legal Theory', which we have taken as the title of the present work. A perfectly literal translation would have required 'legal science' in the title instead of 'legal theory'. (See also the Translators' Preface, above.)

2. 'Legal policy' ('*Rechtspolitik*'), § 1, n. 2. In the present text, Kelsen's interest in legal policy is largely negative. He deplores what he sees as confusion between 'is' and 'ought', confusion between the posited law and *de lege ferenda* (or law that ought to be posited). The latter falls under the rubric of legal policy, standing in sharp contrast to legal science.

In Austrian economics, the same juxtaposition, accompanied by the same expression of concern over the same sort of confusion, is found in Carl Menger's treatise of 1883. Criticizing the Historical School of economics (Karl Knies, Gustav Schmoller) for failing to distinguish a specifically historical understanding of economics from theoretical economics (a criticism that would give rise to the great *Methodenstreit* of the late nineteenth century), Menger continues:

> Every bit as serious a mistake about the nature of theoretical economics (*theoretische Nationalökonomie*) and its position within the social sciences is made by those who confuse it with *economic policy* (*Volkswirtschaftspolitik*), who confuse the science of the general nature and relations of economic phenomena with the science of purposeful maxims for directing and advancing the economy.

Carl Menger, *Investigations into the Method of the Social Sciences with Special Reference to Economics*, trans. Francis J. Nock (New York: New York UP, 1985), 46 (Menger's italics). (The passage quoted is our own translation from the German-language text.)

Menger's reference to 'purposeful maxims' invites attention to a point helpful in understanding 'legal policy': the concern over appropriate or effective means to an end. Kelsen's own abiding interest in questions of legal policy illustrates the point. Given the end, say, of constraining the exercise of legislative power, what are the most appropriate or effective means thereto? In his important and provocative reply to Carl Schmitt on the question 'Who Shall Be the Guardian of the Constitution?', Kelsen makes the case for a central constitutional court. The issue, in Kelsen's view, is one of legal policy, not legal science. See Kelsen, 'Wer soll der Hüter der Verfassung sein?', *Die Justiz*, 6 (1931), 5–56, repr. in *WS II*, 1873–922.

3. 'Human sciences' ('*Geisteswissenschaften*'), § 8, n. 13. The difficulty in rendering '*Geisteswissenschaft*' stems from the fact that neither of its components, '*Wissenschaft*' and '*Geist*', has a close English-language counterpart. The very considerable difference between '*Wissenschaft*' and 'science' was underscored by the Heidelberg neo-Kantian, Wilhelm Windelband, when he wrote that the Greek '*philosophia*' means 'exactly what we describe today with the German "*Wissenschaft*", which happily includes a good deal more than the English or French "*science*" '. Windelband, *Präludien*, 2nd edn. (Tübingen: J. C. B. Mohr, 1903), 13. '*Geist*', for its part, can be rendered as 'spirit', 'mind', 'intellect', 'ideal', and even 'ghost', to name but a few possibilities, and the difficulties it has created in translations are notorious. The following rendition of a line from Kelsen (translated as a quotation in an essay by Otto Neurath) illustrates the point:

> [T]he state, as the object of a special mode of thought to be distinguished from psychology, is a distinctive reality . . . resid[ing] not in the realm of *nature*—the realm of physical–psychical relations—but in the realm of spirit (*Geist*).

Neurath, 'Sociology and Physicalism', trans. Morton Magnus and Ralph Raico, in *Logical Positivism*, ed. A.J. Ayer (Glencoe, Ill.: Free Press, 1959), 282–317, at 307, quoting from Kelsen's *Allgemeine Staatslehre* (Berlin: Springer, 1925, repr. Bad Homburg v. d. Höhe: Max Gehlen, 1966), at 14. Kelsen's contrast, here, is between an *ideal* realm and the *natural* realm, the realm of nature. (See also § 8, text at n. 12.)

Windelband's successor at Heidelberg, Heinrich Rickert, contending that the term '*Geisteswissenschaft*' was so laden with psychical connotations that its use led only to confusion, introduced 'cultural science' ('*Kulturwissenschaft*') to take its place. See Rickert, *Science and History* (1st pub. 1899), trans. George Reisman (Princeton, NJ: D. Van Nostrand, 1962), at pp. xiv–xv, 11, 22–3, 80–103, *et passim*. For Kelsen, Rickert's cure was worse than the disease;

Rickert's notion of cultural science, Kelsen contended, simply marks yet another distinction within the field of the physical or explanatory sciences, thereby leaving unaddressed the question of a distinction between the physical sciences and the human sciences or *Geisteswissenschaften*. In Kelsen's words:

> It is well known that Rickert sought to work out uncompromisingly the contrast between *nature* and *culture* in order to use the contrast as the basis for a new system of the sciences. The division into natural science and cultural science, however, applies simply to the physical or explanatory sciences. In spite of the different objects of cognition and different methods that distinguish natural science and cultural science, they stand on common ground: the causal explanation of reality.

Kelsen, 'Die Rechtswissenschaft als Norm- oder als Kulturwissenschaft', *Schmollers Jahrbuch für Gesetzgebung, Verwaltung und Volkswirtschaft im Deutschen Reiche*, 40 (1916), 1181–239, at 1184, repr. in *WS I*, 37–93, at 40.

Kelsen himself, however, had never been content with the notion of *Geisteswissenschaft* either, and he in fact rarely appeals to it. (His use of '*Geisteswissenschaft*' in § 8 of the present text is one such rarity.) He prefers a distinction between *normative sciences* and *natural sciences*:

> The contrast between 'is' and 'ought' is dispositive for distinguishing in principle all the sciences. . . . The division into *explicative* and *normative* disciplines, into sciences of causality and of norms, is based on the contrast between 'is' and 'ought'. The disciplines of the one are directed to that which is actually given, to the world of the 'is', to *reality*, whereas the disciplines of the other turn their consideration to the world of the 'ought', of *ideality*.

Kelsen, *Über Grenzen zwischen juristischer und soziologischer Methode* (Tübingen: J. C. B. Mohr, 1911), 10–11, repr. in *WS I*, 3–36, at 8–9 (Kelsen's italics). This statement, in which the contrast between 'is' and 'ought' is put to work as dispositive in distinguishing in principle between natural and normative sciences, which are directed to *real* and *ideal* spheres respectively, is characteristic of Kelsen's early work. One source of the dichotomy of 'real' vs. 'ideal' is Windelband, *Präludien*, op. cit. 257; cp. Kelsen, *HP* 4 (citing Windelband's text).

4. 'Idea of law' ('*Rechtsidee*'), § 10, n. 18. See also § 13. In the German-language literature, 'idea of law' is often treated as

synonymous with 'justice'. Thus, Julius Binder defines the idea of law by quoting Kant's lines on justice at the end of section B in Kant's Introduction to the *Rechtslehre*. See Binder, *Philosophie des Rechts*, 1st edn. (Berlin: Georg Stilke, 1925, repr. Aalen: Scientia, 1967), at 257.

A second, related approach is to treat 'idea of law' as simply another label for natural law theory. Karl Bergbohm, for example, dismisses the expression 'idea of law' with the suggestion that its use marks an attempt to 'disguise a timorous version of natural law'. Bergbohm, *Jurisprudenz und Rechtsphilosophie* (Leipzig: Duncker & Humblot, 1892, repr. Glashütten im Taunus: Detlev Auvermann, 1973), 295.

An influential modern development is Gustav Radbruch's argument that an explication of the idea of law in terms of justice, fine as far as it goes, is incomplete. His reason is the familiar one. 'Justice demands, to be sure, that those who are alike be treated alike and those who are different be treated in accordance with their differences, but it leaves open the questions of whom to consider alike, whom different, and how to treat them.' Radbruch, *Legal Philosophy* (1st pub. 1932), trans. Kurt Wilk, in *The Legal Philosophies of Lask, Radbruch, and Dabin*, intro. by Edwin W. Patterson (Cambridge, Mass.: Harvard UP, 1950), 90–1. The idea of law is incomplete without a second element, the element of purpose. Radbruch does not have in mind the statements of purpose that turn up in the course of legal interpretation. Rather, he is looking to what he calls the 'supra-empirical idea of purpose', the 'ultimate end of social life'—liberty in the 'individualist' view of law, nation in the 'supra-individualist' view, and culture in the 'transpersonal' view. The supra-empirical purpose reflects an outlook on life or *Lebens-anschauung*, and provides values for the variables in the formal scheme of justice. Finally, a third element of the idea of law, legal certainty, is often at odds with justice. The result is internal tension—Radbruch speaks of antinomies—within the idea of law (see ibid., at 108–12).

5. 'Reconstructed legal norm' ('*Rechtssatz*'), § 11(*b*), n. 20. 'Reconstructed legal norm', 'basic form of positive laws' (see § 11(*b*), text at n. 21), and 'legal norm in its primary form' (see § 14(*b*), text at n. 25) are all expressions reflecting Kelsen's answer in the present work to the question of the 'ideal form' of the legal norm:

> The question of whether the legal norm is to be viewed as an imperative or as a hypothetical judgment [namely, that a sanction be attached to certain behaviour] is the question of the *ideal* linguistic form of the legal norm or, rather, the question of the

nature of the objective law. The reading that is used in practice in concrete legal systems is irrelevant to the resolution of the problem. The legal norm (in its ideal form) must be constructed from the content of statutes, and the components needed for the construction are often not present in one and the same statute but must be assembled from several statutes.

HP 237 (Kelsen's italics).

Kelsen enquires into the 'ideal form' of the legal norm as part of his effort to distinguish legal norms from norms of morality. Earlier theorists had argued that both legal and moral norms have the same imperative form, a view Kelsen believes to be mistaken and a source of confusion generally about the law and morality.

In his early writings, Kelsen defends a theory on 'ideal form' according to which the imperative 'Do X!', addressed to the legal subject, is necessarily linked with a hypothetical judgment, addressed to the official: 'If not X, then a certain sanction ought to be imposed'. (See *HP*, at 235–6.) In the present text, the imperative becomes a 'secondary norm', secondary to the hypothetical judgment, the 'legal norm in its primary form'. (See § 14(*b*).) And it is to this reconstructed legal norm, thus understood, that Kelsen refers with the expression '*Rechtssatz*'.

Eugenio Bulygin usefully renders '*Rechtssatz*' as one type of 'reconstruction of a norm', referring to the German text of the present work. We have followed his rendition in our translation. See Bulygin, 'Zur Problem der Anwendbarkeit der Logik auf das Recht', in *Festschrift für Ulrich Klug zum 70. Geburtstag*, ed. Günter Kohlmann, vol. i (Cologne: Peter Deubner, 1983), 19–31, at 20; also in Spanish under the title 'Sobre el problema de la aplicabilidad de la lógica al derecho', trans. Jerónimo Betegón, in Hans Kelsen and Ulrich Klug, *Normas jurídicas y análisis lógico* (Madrid: Centro de Estudios Constitucionales, 1988), 9–26, at 11.

Apart from Kelsen's quasi-technical use of '*Rechtssatz*' in the present work, the expression is used in a multitude of texts in legal theory, and in the various fields of the substantive law, typically as a mere synonym for '*Rechtsnorm*' ('legal norm'). One illustration here stems from Georg Puchta: 'the individual legal norms (*Rechtssätze*) that form the law of a people are organically related to one another . . .' Puchta, *Cursus der Institutionen*, 10th edn., vol. i (Leipzig: Breitkopf & Härtel, 1893), 21. (See also the quotation from Paul Laband in n. 14 of the Introduction to the present text.) A second illustration stems from Rudolf von Jhering, who in his early, conceptual period addresses himself to the question of the formation of law:

One sees that something occurs, then recurs again and again, one feels that it must occur, and one gives verbal expression to this 'must'. So it is that legal norms (*Rechtssätze*) come into being.

Jhering, *Geist des römischen Rechts*, vol. i, 2nd edn. (Leipzig: Breitkopf & Härtel, 1866), 28.

In his later writings, Kelsen introduces '*Rechtssatz*' as the propositional counterpart of a legal norm. For example, in the second edition of the *Reine Rechtslehre* or *Pure Theory of Law* (see Translators' Preface to the present text, n. 6), he contends that the proper task of legal science is to describe legal norms and the relations constituted by them:

> The propositions that legal science uses to describe these relations must be distinguished, as legal *propositions* (*Rechtssätze*), from legal *norms* (*Rechtsnormen*), which are created and to be applied by legal organs and are to be followed by legal subjects. Legal *propositions* are hypothetical judgments stating that in terms of a . . . legal system, certain conditions, as determined by the system, ought to lead to certain consequences, as determined by the system. Legal *norms* are not judgments, that is, they are not statements about an object given to cognition.

Ibid. § 16 (Kelsen's italics). This later distinction of Kelsen's between legal norm and legal proposition is not evident in the present text, notwithstanding the fact that his distinction between the law and legal science is made abundantly clear—is, indeed, a leitmotiv of the book.

6. 'Imputation' ('*Zurechnung*'), § 11(*b*), n. 22. On peripheral imputation, see § 11(*b*); on central imputation, see §§ 25(*a*)–(*b*),(*d*)–(*e*), 48(*a*)–(*b*). The more prominent notion in Kelsen's work, save for the early writings, is peripheral imputation, understood as the attribution of a material fact (say, a delict) to a legal person *qua* legal subject, whereby the subject's legal liability is established. Peripheral imputation may be seen as a rough legal analogue to the concept of moral imputation familiar from Kant and others in the philosophical tradition. See Kant's *Rechtslehre*, trans. John Ladd under the title *The Metaphysical Elements of Justice* (Indianapolis, Ind.: Library of Liberal Arts, 1965), at 29; and Leonard Nelson, *System of Ethics* (1st pub. 1932), trans. Norbert Guterman (New Haven, Conn.: Yale UP, 1956), at 55. In his later writings, Kelsen, too, speaks of moral imputation; see e.g. Kelsen, *What Is Justice?* (Berkeley, Calif.: University of California Press, 1957), at 333–4. On the concept of imputation generally, see Joachim Hruschka, 'Imputation', *Brigham Young University Law Review* (1986), 669–710, a rich and suggestive paper.

In the present text, representative of Kelsen's neo-Kantian phase, he sees peripheral imputation as providing the peculiarly non-causal or normative link between a material fact as condition (delict) and another material fact as consequence (punishment), and he hints at how—in the guise of a neo-Kantian argument—the case for this link and for the resulting liability of the legal subject might be made. Even if Kelsen's neo-Kantian alternative is found wanting (as argued in the Introduction, above, at pp. xxix–xlii), the significance for Kelsen of peripheral imputation *qua* 'principle of normativity' cannot be overestimated. See, in addition to § 11(*b*) of the present text, Kelsen, *General Theory of Law and State* (Cambridge, Mass.: Harvard UP, 1945), at 46.

Central imputation is a key notion in Kelsen's very early works (see, above all, *HP*, at 121–46, 183–7, *et passim*). Here he has in mind the attribution of an act to a legal person *qua* norm complex (say, the state)—to a 'point of imputation', as Kelsen terms it— whereby the legal character of the act is established. Nineteenth-century volitional or 'will' theorists of law had argued that the legal character of an act turned on showing the act to be, *inter alia*, a manifestation of the will of the state, and Kelsen's notion of central imputation, obviating any appeal to a 'psychical' notion of will, is a part of his general reply to these theorists.

'*Zurechnung*' has been rendered by Kelsen's translators not only as 'imputation' but also as 'ascription' and 'accounting'. One consideration in favour of 'imputation', our preferred reading generally, is Kelsen's own usage, namely, his occasional substitution of various forms of the verb '*imputieren*' for '*zurechnen*' (see e.g. *HP*, at 138, 194, 209, 503).

A second consideration in favour of 'imputation' as the preferred rendition of '*Zurechnung*' stems from translators' interpretations of texts from the Austrian School of economics. Friedrich von Wieser took over the legal notion of *Zurechnung*, introducing it into economics as a means of marking the phenomenon by which individuals' subjective valuations serve to attribute or *impute* values to the goods in question. Wieser, *Der natürliche Werth* (Vienna: Hölder, 1889), 70–6, trans. Christian A. Malloch under the title *Natural Value* (London: Macmillan, 1893, repr. New York: Kelly & Millman, 1956), 72–8. In English-language translations of texts by Wieser, Carl Menger, Hans Meyer, and more recently Friedrich A. Hayek, '*Zurechnung*' is rendered as 'imputation'; see e.g. 'Some Remarks on the Problem of Imputation', in Hayek, *Money, Capital, and Fluctuations. Early Essays*, ed. Roy McCloughry (London: Routledge & Kegan Paul, 1984), 33–54, originally appearing as 'Bemerkungen zum Zurechnungsproblem', *Jahrbücher für National-ökonomie und Statistik*, 69 (1926), 1–18.

7. 'Jurisprudence of concepts' ('*Begriffsjurisprudenz*' or '*Konstruktionsjurisprudenz*'), §39, n. 62. Although Freidrich Carl von Savigny, in his early Marburg 'Lectures on Legal Method' (1802–3), lent his programmatic endorsement to both the systematic and the historical approach, later Romanists, profoundly influenced by Roman law constructivism, inclined toward a narrower, more systematic approach. The view, often termed *Begriffsjurisprudenz* or—more useful in pointing to its Roman law source—*Konstruktionsjurisprudenz*, is associated above all with the Romanists Georg Puchta and, in his earlier phase, Rudolf von Jhering.

There is no better guide to *Begriffsjurisprudenz* than Jhering. He begins his career as a convinced proponent of the view, but grows increasingly disenchanted with it, offering a sharp-witted critique of the theory and ultimately rejecting it outright.

The first volume of *Geist des römischen Rechts* (see Supplementary Note 5, above), or *The Spirit of the Roman Law*, reflects Jhering's position in his early, constructivist phase. Drawing on 'the prevailing view of the law as an objective organism', Jhering distinguishes 'anatomical' and 'physiological' points of view. The 'anatomical' point of view provides for a structural analysis, with an eye to identifying legal norms abstracted from the general fabric of human relations. The 'physiological' point of view provides for a functional analysis, with an eye to distinguishing certain legal norms by a common function or purpose, and bringing them together in legal institutes representing 'functional' aggregates. Jhering, ibid. 25–8. The legal material in question, Jhering continues, is not only to be identified and ordered; it must also be 'reduced to logical elements of the system'. And logical reduction, a task of legal theory, is aimed at 'forming new concepts and new legal norms'. Ibid. 40.

Later, in writings after 1861, Jhering begins to dismantle his own constructivist system and takes to twitting his former allies, the constructivists. The first of a number of letters originally published anonymously in a newspaper for jurists opens with these lines:

> You know the tale of that mischievous devil who raised rooftops to let his protégé peek into the secrets of the rooms below. Allow me to take over his role once and show you the workrooms of our legal theorists. In the stillness of the night, you see here by lamplight those who shoulder legal scholarship, busy at work, the *corpus juris* close at hand, this mine of civil law wisdom. What are they up to? I wager that half of them—at least the younger ones, the hope of Germany—are at this very moment *constructing*. What is construction? Fifty years ago no one knew a thing about it, one 'lived innocently, contentedly, levelling one's

artillery only at Pandectist positions'. How dramatically things have changed! Now, whoever isn't in the know about 'civil law construction' will see how he gets by; just as a lady wouldn't dare to appear these days without her petticoat, so likewise for a modern civil lawyer without his construction. I don't know who is responsible for this new fashion in civil law. All I know is that someone ·has even reconstructed construction itself and given special directions for it—indeed, in order to go about his project, has even built an upper storey of jurisprudence, which has been named, accordingly, 'higher jurisprudence'.

'Die civilistische Konstruktion', first appearing in the *Preußische Gerichts-Zeitung*, 3/41 (26 June 1861), was reprinted in Jhering, *Scherz und Ernst in der Jurisprudenz* (Leipzig: Breitkopf & Härtel, 1891, repr. Darmstadt: Wiss. Buchgesellschaft, 1980), 3–17, at 6–7.

Appendix II

Biographical Outline*

Hans Kelsen born, 11 Oct. 1881, in Prague. Parents: Adolf (1850–1907) and Auguste (née Löwy, 1860–1950) Kelsen.

Vienna: 1883–1930

1883	Family moves from Prague to Vienna.
1887–91	Hans attends evangelical primary school.
1891–2	Attends public primary school.
1892–1900	Attends classical *Gymnasium*.
1900–1	Serves on active military duty.
1901	Begins law study at University of Vienna.
1905	Publishes *The Political Philosophy of Dante* (Leipzig and Vienna, iv, 152-pp.).
1905–10	Conducts research on problems in the theory of public law (culminating in the treatise *Main Problems*, 1911, below).
1906	Takes doctorate in law.
1908–9	Spends 3 semesters in Heidelberg, conducting research.
1909–10	Lecturer, Export Academy, Vienna.
1911	Publishes *Main Problems in the Theory of Public Law* (Tübingen, xxvii, 709-pp.).
1911	Applies successfully for *Habilitation* (licence to hold university lectures), submitting *Main Problems* as thesis, and is admitted as *Privatdozent* (private lecturer), Faculty of Law, University of Vienna.
1912	Marries Margarete Bondi (2 daughters: Anna, born 1914; Maria, born 1915).
1913	Publishes *On Unlawful Acts of the State* (Vienna, 113-pp.).
1914–18	Establishes and edits the *Austrian Journal of Public Law*, Vienna (3 volumes); Aug. 1914 (World War I): is called to active duty, serves primarily in Ministry of War, Vienna, until Oct. 1918.

* We have drawn on Rudolf Aladár Métall's *Hans Kelsen. Leben und Werk* (Vienna: Franz Deuticke, 1969) for numerous entries.

1918   Oct.: commences work, at behest of Chancellor Karl Renner, on drafting of new Austrian constitution.

1917–19   Associate Professor, Faculty of Law, University of Vienna.

1919–30   Professor, Public and Administrative Law, University of Vienna.

1919   Establishes and edits the *Journal of Public Law*, Vienna (23 volumes running to 1944, Kelsen plays no role after 1934).

1920   Publishes *The Problem of Sovereignty* (Tübingen, x, 320-pp.); publishes *Socialism and the State* (Leipzig, iv, 129-pp.); publishes *On the Nature and Value of Democracy* (Tübingen, 38-pp.); 1 Oct.: Austrian Federal Constitution, in whose conception and drafting Kelsen played a major role, is adopted.

1921   Kelsen is appointed to Constitutional Court for 'life term'.

1922   Edits monograph series 'Vienna Studies in Constitutional Law and Politics' (Kelsen active to 1929); publishes *Sociological and Legal Concepts of the State* (Tübingen, iv, 253-pp.); publishes *Legal Science and the Law* (Leipzig and Vienna, 135-pp.).

1923   Publishes *Austrian Constitutional Law* (Tübingen, viii, 256-pp.).

1925   Publishes *General Political Theory* (Berlin, xiv, 433-pp.).

1926   29–30 Mar.: responds to Erich Kaufmann at meeting of the Association of German Teachers of Public Law, Münster; establishes, with Franz Weyr and Léon Duguit, the bilingual (French and German) *International Journal for Legal Theory*, Brno, Czechoslovakia (13 volumes running to 1939); delivers Hague Lectures, Academy of International Law (Kelsen's first Hague Lecture series).

1926–8   Dispensation cases reach the Constitutional Court. (Courts of general jurisdiction had held that administrative authorities' dispensations, permitting remarriage in Roman Catholic Austria, were invalid. These judicial rulings are overturned by the Constitutional Court, with Kelsen taking the lead. The Christian Social Party is prompted to take steps leading to 'constitutional reform' and, by means of it, the ouster of Kelsen from the Court, 1930, below.)

1927   24–5 Mar.: Kelsen responds to Max Wenzel and Hermann Heller at meeting of the Association of German Teachers of Public Law, Munich.

1928	23–4 Apr.: delivers main paper, 'Nature and Development of Judicial Review', at meeting of the Association of German Teachers of Public Law, Vienna.
1929	25–6 Apr.: participates in meeting of the Association of German Teachers of Public Law, Frankfurt; 7 Dec.: 'constitutional reform', including reorganization of the Constitutional Court, is passed in the Parliament.
1930	15 Feb.: Constitutional Court justices, among them Kelsen, are removed from office as one result of the 'reform'; Kelsen accepts offer of professorship at University of Cologne.

Cologne: 1930–1933

1930–3	Nov.–Apr.: Professor, Public International Law, University of Cologne.
1931	Publishes *Who Shall Be the Guardian of the Constitution?* (Berlin, 56-pp.) in reply to Carl Schmitt.
1932	Delivers Hague Lectures, Academy of International Law (Kelsen's second Hague Lecture series).
1932–3	Dean, Faculty of Law, University of Cologne.
1933	30 Jan.: Nazis seize power in Germany; 7 Apr.: Kelsen is dismissed from his university post, on the authority of the notorious 'Law for the Restoration of the Professional Civil Service', which removes those of Jewish ancestry from their positions in the civil service; spring: the Kelsen family leaves Germany; 10 May: Kelsen is named 'Foreign Honorary Member', American Academy of Arts and Sciences; summer: accepts offer at Graduate Institute for International Legal Studies, Geneva.

Geneva: 1933–1940

1933	Autumn: commences teaching and research in Geneva.
1934	Publishes *Pure Theory of Law*, 1st edn. (Vienna, xxi, 168-pp., and biblio.), the first appearance of the work translated here.
1936	20 Apr.: receives honorary doctorate, University of Utrecht; accepts offer of professorship at Charles University in Prague, to be held jointly with appointment in Geneva; 18 Sept.: receives honorary doctorate, Harvard University.
1936–7	Winter term: attempts to deliver lectures at Charles University in Prague, but political harassment, including blatant anti-Semitism and threats on Kelsen's life, makes it impossible.
1939	Resolves to leave Europe.

| 1940 | May: departs from Geneva. |

America: 1940–1973

1940	21 June: Hans and Margarete Kelsen arrive in New York.
1940–2	Kelsen works as 'research associate' at Harvard Law School, with stipend from the Rockefeller Foundation.
1940–1	Delivers Oliver Wendell Holmes Lectures, Harvard Law School, published in 1942 as *Law and Peace in International Relations* (Cambridge, Mass., xi, 181-pp.).
1941	Sept.: receives honorary doctorate, University of Chicago.
1942	Spring term: Mary Whiton Calkins Professor, Wellesley College.
1942–5	Autumn–spring: visiting lectureship, Department of Political Science, University of California, Berkeley.
1944	Publishes *Peace through Law* (Chapel Hill, NC, xii, 155-pp.).
1945	Publishes *General Theory of Law and State* (Cambridge, Mass., xxxiii, 388-pp., and appendix); spring–summer: legal adviser, United Nations War Crimes Commission, Washington, DC.
1945–52	Professor, Department of Political Science, University of California, Berkeley.
1946	Publishes *Society and Nature* (London, viii, 391-pp.).
1947	24 June: is named 'honorary professor', University of Vienna.
1949	25 June: is named 'honorary professor', University of Rio de Janeiro; publishes *Political Theory of Bolshevism. A Critical Study* (Berkeley, iv, 60-pp.).
1950	Publishes *Law of the United Nations* (London, xvii, 903-pp.).
1951	21 July: receives honorary doctorate, National University of Mexico.
1952	28 Jan.: receives honorary doctorate, University of California, Berkeley; publishes *Principles of International Law* (New York, xvii, 461-pp.); delivers valedictory lecture, 'What is Justice?', University of California, Berkeley.
1952–3	Visiting Professor, Graduate Institute for International Legal Studies, Geneva.
1953	Delivers Hague Lectures, Academy of International Law (Kelsen's third Hague Lecture series).
1953–4	Visiting Professor of International Law, United States Naval War College, Newport, Rhode Island.

1954	Receives honorary doctorate, University of Salamanca (Spain).
1955	Publishes *Communist Theory of Law* (London, viii, 203-pp.); publishes *Foundations of Democracy* (Chicago, 101-pp.), a version of Walgreen Lectures, University of Chicago.
1957	Publishes *Collective Security under International Law* (Washington, DC, vi, 275-pp.); publishes *What is Justice?* (Berkeley, 397-pp.), a collection of papers.
1959–71	(approx.) Conducts research on the theory of norms, the work of his 'later period', marked by scepticism and tacit defence of 'will' theory of law.
1960	5 Apr.: is named 'honorary professor', National University of Mexico; 9 June: is awarded the prestigious 'Premio Feltrinelli', Italian Academy of the Lincei; publishes *Pure Theory of Law*, 2nd edn. (Vienna, xii, 498-pp.).
1961	20 July: receives honorary doctorate, Free University of Berlin; 18 Sept.: receives honorary doctorate, University of Vienna; 27 Sept.: receives honorary doctorate, New School for Social Research, New York.
1963	7 Nov.: receives honorary doctorate, University of Paris.
1967	1 June: receives honorary doctorate, University of Salzburg.
1973	19 Apr.: Kelsen's death, Berkeley, California.
1979	*General Theory of Norms* (xii, 362-pp.) is published in Vienna.
1985	*The Illusion of Justice. A Critical Examination of Plato's Social Philosophy* (x, 485-pp.) is published in Vienna.

Appendix III

Short Annotated Bibliography of Secondary Literature in English

The secondary literature on Kelsen is vast. I have divided the brief selection below into six groups, listing in each group items that may be helpful in connection with the themes and problems of the present treatise. (Still other secondary literature is cited in the Supplementary Notes, appendix I.)

Group I. Writings by Recent and Contemporary Philosophers

The best writings on philosophers are very often the works of other philosophers, and philosophers' writings on Kelsen underscore the point. See e.g. H. L. A. Hart, 'Kelsen Visited', *UCLA Law Review*, 10 (1962–3), 709–28, repr. in Hart, *Essays in Jurisprudence and Philosophy* (Oxford: Clarendon Press, 1983), 283–308. (A second essay by Hart on Kelsen is listed below, in group VI.) Although Hart pays Kelsen relatively little close attention in *The Concept of Law* (Oxford: Clarendon Press, 1961), much in the book reflects Kelsen's profound influence. For Hart's criticism of Kelsenian doctrines, see *The Concept of Law*, 35–41, 238–40 (on the hypothetically formulated legal norm), and 105–6, 228–31, 245–7, 256–7 (on the basic norm); on Hart's criticism, see J. T. Cameron, 'Observations on *The Concept of Law*', *Juridical Review*, 8 N.S. (1963), 101–16.

Joseph Raz considers Kelsen at length in *The Concept of a Legal System*, 2nd edn. (Oxford: Clarendon Press, 1980); this work, together with Raz's *Practical Reason and Norms*, 2nd edn. (Princeton, NJ: Princeton UP, 1990), and *The Authority of Law* (Oxford: Clarendon Press, 1979), provides the most complete and accessible general statement on normativism extant, with a substantial critique of Kelsen. See also Raz's papers 'The Purity of the Pure Theory', *Revue Internationale de Philosophie*, 35 (1981), 441–59, repr. in *Essays on Kelsen*, ed. Richard Tur and William Twining (Oxford: Clarendon

Press, 1986), 79–97; and 'The Problem about the Nature of Law', in *Contemporary Philosophy. A New Survey*, vol. iii, ed. Guttorm Fløistad (The Hague: Nijhoff, 1982), 107–25, esp. 113–16, repr. *University of Western Ontario Law Review*, 21 (1983), 203–18, esp. 208–10.

The Danish legal philosopher Alf Ross (1899–1979), once a student of Kelsen's in Vienna, considers Kelsen at several points in *On Law and Justice*, trans. Margaret Dutton (London: Stevens & Sons, 1958); more generally, the book is valuable as a (highly critical) insider's view of Kelsenian themes. See also Ross's earlier treatise, *Towards a Realistic Jurisprudence*, trans. Annie I. Fausbøll (Copenhagen: Einar Munksgaard, 1946, repr. Aalen: Scientia, 1989), and his scathing review of Kelsen's *What Is Justice?*, in the *California Law Review*, 45 (1957), 564–70. Finally, see Ross's paper, 'Validity and the Conflict between Legal Positivism and Natural Law', *Revista jurídica de Buenos Aires*, 4 (1961), 46–93, and his monograph *Directives and Norms* (London: Routledge & Kegan Paul, 1968), at 156–8. (On Ross, see also group VI below.)

The Swedish legal philosopher Axel Hägerström (1868–1939) wrote an important review article on Kelsen's *Allgemeine Staatslehre* (1925); the paper first appeared in 1928, and was translated in a volume of Hägerström's studies in legal philosophy, *Inquiries into the Nature of Law and Morals*, trans. C. D. Broad (Uppsala: Almqvist & Wiksell, 1953), 257–98.

The Italian legal and political philosopher Norberto Bobbio has written on Kelsen and, indeed, played a central role in the reception accorded to Kelsen in post-War Italy. See Bobbio's valuable paper ' "Sein" and "Sollen" in Legal Science', in *Sein und Sollen im Erfahrungsbereich des Rechtes*, ed. Peter Schneider (Wiesbaden: Franz Steiner, 1970), 7–31, which is largely devoted to Kelsen; see also Bobbio, 'Law and Force', *Monist*, 49 (1965), 321–41. (Although several volumes of Bobbio's political theory have recently appeared in English, very little of his work in legal philosophy has been translated.)

The American moral philosopher Alan Gewirth has written on Kelsen in the paper 'The Quest for Specificity in Jurisprudence', *Ethics*, 69 (1959), 155–81. Earlier, the logical positivist Gustav Bergmann wrote, together with Lewis Zerby, on 'The Formalism of Kelsen's Pure Theory of Law', *Ethics*, 55 (1945), 110–30.

*Group II. Older Writings by Academic Lawyers,
Including Émigrés from Central Europe*

Group II brings together a number of older papers, excerpts from books, and a single monograph. Some of these writers are European scholars of law and politics who had studied in Vienna (Lauterpacht, Voegelin, Akzin, Ebenstein, Kunz) and then emigrated to the English-speaking world (Lauterpacht and Voegelin in the 1920s, Akzin, Ebenstein, and Kunz in the early 1930s, with Akzin finally settling in Israel). Their writings, some highly critical, are of special value as statements of the views of insiders. (Alf Ross, as noted above, qualifies on both counts.) Other insiders include Kelsen's own colleagues in the Vienna School, Adolf Julius Merkl and Alfred Verdross (see groups V and VI respectively), and the international lawyer Leo Gross (see group VI).

William Ebenstein's monograph *The Pure Theory of Law*, trans. Charles H. Wilson (Madison, Wis.: University of Wisconsin Press, 1945, repr. New York: Rothman, 1969), is especially helpful as one estimate of the Kantian dimension in Kelsen's theory. See also Ebenstein's article-length statements, 'Kelsen, Hans', *International Encyclopedia of the Social Sciences*, vol. viii (1967), 360–6, and 'The Pure Theory of Law: Demythologizing Legal Thought', *California Law Review*, 59 (1971), 617–52. (See group III below for other views on the Kantian dimension.)

All of the following are suggestive on aspects of Kelsen's early writings: Erich Voegelin, 'Kelsen's Pure Theory of Law', *Political Science Quarterly*, 42 (1927), 268–76; Rupert Emerson, *State and Sovereignty in Modern Germany* (New Haven, Conn.: Yale UP, 1928), 167–79; Johannes Mattern, *Concepts of State, Sovereignty and International Law* (Baltimore: Johns Hopkins Press, and London: Oxford UP, 1928), 121–39; Frederick Hallis, *Corporate Personality. A Study in Jurisprudence* (London: Oxford UP, 1930), 49–60; Hersch Lauterpacht, 'Kelsen's Pure Science of Law', in *Modern Theories of Law*, intro. by W. Ivor Jennings (London: Oxford UP, 1933), 105–38; Josef L. Kunz, 'The "Vienna School" and International Law', *New York University Law Quarterly Review*, 11 (1934), 370–421 (which offers a general statement at 370–92); Charles H. Wilson, 'The Basis of Kelsen's Theory of Law', *Politica*, 1 (1934), 54–82; Henry Janzen, 'Kelsen's Theory of Law', *American Political Science Review*, 31 (1937), 205–26; Isaac Husik, 'The Legal Philosophy of Hans Kelsen', *Journal of Social Philosophy*, 3 (1938), 297–324, repr. in Husik, *Philosophical Essays*, ed. Milton C. Nahm and Leo Strauss (Oxford: Basil Blackwell, 1952), 292–321; Lon L. Fuller, *The Law in Quest of Itself* (Chicago, Ill.: Foundation Press, 1940, repr. Boston: Beacon Press, 1966), 66–77; Kurt Wilk, 'Law and the State as Pure Ideas: Critical Notes on the Basic Concepts of Kelsen's Legal Philosophy', *Ethics*, 51 (1941), 158–84; and Benjamin Akzin, 'Analysis of State and Law Structure', in *Law, State, and International Legal Order. Essays in Honor of Hans Kelsen*, ed. Salo Engel (Knoxville, Tenn.: University of

Tennessee Press, 1964), 1–20. In a more personal vein, see Akzin, 'Hans Kelsen—*In Memoriam*', *Israel Law Review*, 8 (1973), 325–9.

See, too, Julius Stone's chapter on Kelsen in *Legal System and Lawyer's Reasonings* (London: Stevens & Sons, 1964), 98–136, of interest not least of all because Kelsen saw fit to reply (and at length!): see his paper, 'Professor Stone and the Pure Theory of Law', *Stanford Law Review*, 17 (1965), 1128–57. Although Kelsen was defending a 'will' theory of law in the mid–1960s, his reply to Stone is largely a restatement of views antedating the post–1960 shift.

Group III. *Recent Writings by Academic Lawyers and Professional Philosophers*

To appreciate the variety of interpretations of, and puzzles surrounding, Kelsen's basic norm, see e.g. J. W. Harris, *Law and Legal Science* (Oxford: Clarendon Press, 1979), 70–92 *et passim*, who draws on Kelsen's basic norm in developing a 'basic legal science *fiat*'; Torstein Eckhoff and Nils Kristian Sundby, 'The Notion of Basic Norm(s) in Jurisprudence', *Scandinavian Studies in Law*, 19 (1975), 121–51; Aleksander Peczenik, 'On the Nature and Function of the *Grundnorm*', in *Methodologie und Erkenntnistheorie der juristischen Argumentation*, ed. Aulis Aarnio *et al.* (Berlin: Duncker & Humblot, 1981), 279–96; and A. M. Honoré, 'The Basic Norm of a Society', in Honoré, *Making Law Bind* (Oxford: Clarendon Press, 1987), 89–114. (On the basic norm generally, see also the first papers listed on normativity, below.)

A number of papers in the late 1960s and early 1970s on the question of the legitimacy of the revolutionary regime in Rhodesia gave special attention, in that connection, to Kelsen's basic norm; see e.g. R. W. M. Dias, 'Legal Politics: Norms behind the *Grundnorm*', *Cambridge Law Journal*, 26 (1968), 233–59; J. M. Eekelaar, 'Principles of Revolutionary Legality', in *Oxford Essays in Jurisprudence*, 2nd ser., ed. A. W. B. Simpson (Oxford: Clarendon Press, 1973), 22–43; and, in the same volume, J. M. Finnis, 'Revolutions and Continuity of Law', 44–76.

On the nature of legal norms, an intractable problem in Kelsen's theory, an important paper is Carlos E. Alchourrón and Eugenio Bulygin, 'The Expressive Conception of Norms', in *New Studies in Deontic Logic*, ed. Risto Hilpinen (Dordrecht: Reidel, 1981), 95–124. See also Harald Ofstad, 'The Descriptive Definition of the Concept "Legal Norm" Proposed by Hans Kelsen', *Theoria*, 16 (1950), 118–51, 211–46; Ronald Moore, *Legal Norms and Legal Science* (Honolulu: University Press of Hawaii, 1978); Ota Weinberger, 'The Norm as Thought and as Reality', in Neil MacCormick and Ota Weinberger, *An Institutional Theory of Law* (Dordrecht: Reidel, 1986), 31–48; and

Michael Hartney, 'Introduction: the Final Form of the Pure Theory of Law', in Kelsen, *General Theory of Norms*, trans. Michael Hartney (Oxford: Clarendon Press, 1991), pp. ix–liii, esp. xx–liii, where Hartney traces the development of Kelsen's theory of norms from the present book (1934) to the *General Theory of Norms* (first appearing in 1979).

On the problem of normativity, see especially Raz, cited in group I above; particularly instructive on Kelsen's views are Raz's papers 'Kelsen's Theory of the Basic Norm', in *The Authority of Law*, op. cit. 122–45, esp. 134–45, and 'The Purity of the Pure Theory', in *Essays on Kelsen*, op. cit. In their essay 'Normative Positivism: The Mirage of the Middle Way', *Oxford Journal of Legal Studies*, 9 (1989), 463–512, Deryck Beyleveld and Roger Brownsword argue that the 'middle way' defended by both Kelsen and Hart is incoherent. Perspectives on normativity that are addressed primarily to Hart but that apply, *mutatis mutandis*, to Kelsen too, may be found in Philip Soper, *A Theory of Law* (Cambridge, Mass.: Harvard UP, 1984), 26–38; N. E. Simmonds, *Central Issues in Jurisprudence* (London: Sweet & Maxwell, 1986), 91–4; and Gerald J. Postema, 'The Normativity of Law', in *Issues in Contemporary Legal Philosophy*, ed. Ruth Gavison (Oxford: Clarendon Press, 1987), 81–104. Problems of normativity in the work of Hart, Kelsen, and Raz are examined in Jeffrey D. Goldsworthy, 'The Self-Destruction of Legal Positivism', *Oxford Journal of Legal Studies*, 10 (1990), 449–86; and in M. J. Detmold, *The Unity of Law and Morality* (London: Routledge & Kegan Paul, 1984), 32–3, 51–60, 159–60.

The titles of the following papers are a fair indication of their content: Martin P. Golding, 'Kelsen and the Concept of "Legal System" ', *Archiv für Rechts- und Sozialphilosophie*, 47 (1961), 355–86, repr. in *More Essays in Legal Philosophy*, ed. Robert S. Summers (Oxford: Basil Blackwell, 1971), 69–100; A. D. Woozley, 'Legal Duties, Offences, and Sanctions', *Mind*, 77 (1968), 461–79; Neil MacCormick, 'Legal Obligation and the Imperative Fallacy', in *Oxford Essays in Jurisprudence*, 2nd ser., op cit. 100–30; Carlos Santiago Nino, 'Some Confusions around Kelsen's Concept of Validity', *Archiv für Rechts- und Sozialphilosophie*, 64 (1978), 357–77; Alida Wilson, 'The Imperative Fallacy in Kelsen's Theory', *Modern Law Review*, 44 (1981), 270–81; Peter Goodrich, 'The Rise of Legal Formalism; or the Defences of Legal Faith', *Legal Studies*, 3 (1983), 248–66; Bernard S. Jackson, 'Kelsen and the Semiotics of Legal Acts', in Jackson, *Semiotics and Legal Theory* (London: Routledge & Kegan Paul, 1985), 225–62, 337–41 (notes); J. W. Harris, 'Kelsen and Normative Consistency', in *Essays on Kelsen*, op. cit. 201–28; and, in the same volume, Inés Weyland, 'Idealism and Realism in Kelsen's Treatment of Norm Conflicts', 249–69.

There is a useful paper by Hendrik J. van Eikema Hommes, 'The

Development of Hans Kelsen's Concept of Legal Norm', in *Rechtssystem und gesellschaftliche Basis bei Hans Kelsen*, ed. Werner Krawietz and Helmut Schelsky (Berlin: Duncker & Humblot, 1984), 159–78, which, despite its title, is wide-ranging. Similarly, Iain Stewart covers a lot of ground in 'The Critical Legal Science of Hans Kelsen', *Journal of Law and Society*, 17 (1990), 273–308. See also R. S. Clark, 'Hans Kelsen's Pure Theory of Law', *Journal of Legal Education*, 22 (1969–70), 170–96. The main foci of the volume *Hans Kelsen's Legal Theory. A Diachronic Point of View*, ed. Letizia Gianformaggio (Turin: G. Giappichelli Editore, 1990), are a periodization of the Pure Theory, and Kelsen on legal interpretation.

Along with the articles to which reference has already been made, *Essays on Kelsen*, op. cit., contains instructive papers on the Kantian dimension in Kelsen's Pure Theory: see Alida Wilson, 'Is Kelsen Really a Kantian?', 37–64; Iain Stewart, 'Kelsen and the Exegetical Tradition', 123–47; and Richard Tur, 'The Kelsenian Enterprise', 149–83. See also Eugenio Bulygin's statement on competing Kantian and legal positivist themes, in 'An Antinomy in Kelsen's Pure Theory of Law', *Ratio Juris*, 3 (1990), 29–45. Jurisprudence *qua* legal epistemology is discussed by Richard Tur, 'What is Jurisprudence?', *Philosophical Quarterly*, 28 (1978), 149–61, and by Neil MacCormick, 'Analytical Jurisprudence and the Possibility of Legal Knowledge', *Saskatchewan Law Review*, 49 (1985), 1–13, repr. in MacCormick and Weinberger, *An Institutional Theory of Law*, op. cit. 93–109.

Several distinguished comparativists offer some details on the Austrian system of constitutional review, one of Kelsen's major contributions to public law: Mauro Cappelletti, *Judicial Review in the Contemporary World* (Indianapolis, Ind.: Bobbs-Merrill, 1971), 85–96; J. A. C. Grant, 'The Legal Effect of a Ruling that a Statute is Unconstitutional', *Detroit College of Law Review* (1978), 201–39, at 202, 216–19; Allan R. Brewer-Carías, *Judicial Review in Comparative Law* (Cambridge: Cambridge UP, 1989), 185–202, 360–1 (notes). Although Kelsen does not consider details of constitutional review in the present work, everything that he says at § 31(*h*) is germane; for some details on constitutional review, see his paper 'Judicial Review of Legislation. A Comparative Study of the Austrian and the American Constitution', *Journal of Politics*, 4 (1942), 183–200.

Several texts in jurisprudence include useful discussions on Kelsen, of which the most ambitious is Deryck Beyleveld and Roger Brownsword's *Law as a Moral Judgment* (London: Sweet & Maxwell, 1986), 219–78. Roger Cotterrell, in his book *The Politics of Jurisprudence* (London: Butterworths, 1989), at 83–5, 106–17, includes an instructive comparison of Kelsen and Hart. Wide-ranging statements are provided by John D. Finch, *Introduction to Legal Theory*, 3rd edn. (London: Sweet

& Maxwell, 1979), 97–120; by J. W. Harris, *Legal Philosophies* (London: Butterworths, 1980), 59–75; by R. W. M. Dias, *Jurisprudence*, 5th edn. (London: Butterworths, 1985), 358–74; and by Lord Lloyd of Hampstead and M. D. A. Freeman, *Lloyd's Introduction to Jurisprudence*, 5th edn. (London: Stevens & Sons, 1985), 320–47. Two older texts are also helpful on Kelsen: H. F. Jolowicz, *Lectures on Jurisprudence*, ed. J. A. Jolowicz (London: Athlone Press, 1963), 149–59; and Wolfgang Friedmann, *Legal Theory*, 5th edn. (London: Stevens & Sons, 1967), 275–87.

Group IV. Reviews Recording Kelsen's Reception in America

During the first decade of Kelsen's long period in America (from 1940 to his death in 1973), a great many reviews of his book-length works appeared in the law journals; the reader can find them with the help of volumes vi–ix of the *Index to Legal Periodicals* (New York: H. W. Wilson Co.). These reviews record the early reception of Kelsen's work in America, and some are also of interest on the merits. For example, a number of American international lawyers reacted very negatively to much in Kelsen's treatise on the *Law of the United Nations* (London: Stevens & Sons, 1950); legal interpretation was one of the targets of the reviewers' critique, with implications for Kelsen's legal theory generally. See e.g. Louis B. Sohn, Book Review, *Harvard Law Review*, 64 (1950–1), 517–19; Oscar Schachter, Book Review, *Yale Law Journal*, 60 (1951), 189–93; and A. H. Feller, Book Review, *Columbia Law Review*, 51 (1951), 537–9.

Group V. Works Reflecting Basic Assumptions of Continental Legal Theory

Along with direct criticism, another approach to Kelsen is to look at works of originality that offer, *en passant*, perspectives on modern continental legal theory. Alf Ross (see group I above) is a good example. Another is Gustav Radbruch, *Legal Philosophy* (1st pub. 1932), trans. Kurt Wilk, in *The Legal Philosophies of Lask, Radbruch, and Dabin*, intro. by Edwin W. Patterson (Cambridge, Mass.: Harvard UP, 1950), 43–224. Still other useful works in this genre are Karl Olivecrona, *Law as Fact*, 2nd edn. (London: Stevens & Sons, 1971); and Hermann Kantorowicz, *The Definition of Law*, ed. A. H. Campbell (Cambridge: Cambridge UP, 1958). The work of Kelsen's most gifted colleague in the Vienna School, Adolf Julius Merkl, has not been translated into English, save for a long paper 'Prolegomena to a Theory of the Hierarchical

Structure of the Law', forthcoming in *Jurisprudence in Germany and Austria. Selected Modern Themes*, ed. Stanley L. Paulson (Oxford: Clarendon Press).

Also valuable in this genre is the work of comparativists with a penchant for the theoretical; see e.g. George Fletcher, 'The Right and the Reasonable', *Harvard Law Review*, 98 (1984–5), 949–82.

Group VI. Papers on Kelsen's Theory of International Law

The monist–dualist debate in public international law, which Kelsen addresses in Chapter IX of the present text, has not had a great impact in the English-speaking countries. Nevertheless, the theoretical issues have enjoyed attention, not least of all from H. L. A. Hart in his paper 'Kelsen's Doctrine of the Unity of Law', in Hart, *Essays in Jurisprudence and Legal Philosophy*, op. cit. 309–42.

For useful statements of the monism–dualism controversy in texts on public international law, with a fair bit of attention to Kelsen, see D. P. O'Connell, *International Law*, vol. i, 2nd edn. (London: Stevens & Sons, 1970), 38–46; and J. G. Starke, *Introduction to International Law*, 9th edn. (London: Butterworths, 1984), 68–88. Alf Ross, *A Textbook of International Law*, trans. Annie I. Fausbøll (London: Longmans, Green and Co., 1947), 59–73, is of special interest as the work of one who was himself a major figure in legal philosophy. (See group I above.)

Several of the writers in group II above (Emerson, Janzen, Kunz, Lauterpacht, and Mattern) give some attention in the papers listed there to theoretical issues in public international law. See also Hersch Lauterpacht, 'The Nature of International Law and General Jurisprudence', *Economica*, 12 (1932), 301–20, esp. 313–18, on the so-called 'initial hypothesis' (or basic norm) in international law; and J. Walter Jones, 'The "Pure" Theory of International Law', *British Year Book of International Law*, 16 (1935), 5–19. Joseph G. Starke has written two valuable papers, 'Monism and Dualism in the Theory of International Law', *British Year Book of International Law*, 17 (1936), 66–81, and 'The Primacy of International Law', in *Law, State, and International Legal Order*, ed. Engel, op. cit. 307–16, repr. in Starke, *Studies in International Law* (London: Butterworths, 1965), at 1–19 (with supplementary notes), and at 159–67 respectively. Josef L. Kunz's papers, one listed in group II above, and another entitled 'On the Theoretical Basis of the Law of Nations', *Transactions of the Grotius Society*, 10 (1924), 115–42, are helpful statements by a participant in the monist–dualist debate.

Still another paper by Kunz, 'The Problem of the Progressive

Development of International Law', *Iowa Law Review*, 31 (1945–6), 544–60, offers a more general critical perspective on Kelsen's theory of international law. For another insider's general perspective, see Leo Gross, 'States as Organs of International Law and the Problem of Autointerpretation', in *Law and Politics in the World Community*, ed. George A. Lipsky (Berkeley, Calif.: University of California Press, 1953), 59–88, 336–43 (notes), repr. in Gross, *Essays on International Law and Organization*, vol. i (The Hague: Nijhoff, 1984), 367–97. See also the paper by Alfred Verdross, Kelsen's prominent colleague in the Vienna School: 'The Charter of the United Nations and General International Law', in *Law and Politics in the World Community*, op. cit. 153–61, 352–3 (notes).

Further Bibliography

Further references to secondary literature, including items in English, can be found in Rudolf Aladár Métall, *Hans Kelsen. Leben und Werk* (Vienna: Franz Deuticke, 1969), 163–216, and in Horst Dreier, *Rechtslehre, Staatssoziologie und Demokratietheorie bei Hans Kelsen* (Baden-Baden: Nomos, 1986, 2nd printing 1990), 303–28. There is, too, the very useful annotated bibliographical reference work by Michael Dias, *A Bibliography of Jurisprudence*, 3rd edn. (London: Butterworths, 1979), at 260–9.

Finally, where Kelsen's own work is concerned, see Michael Hartney's bibliography of Kelsen's English-language writings (and translations of Kelsen's works into English), listed first alphabetically and then chronologically, in Kelsen, *General Theory of Norms*, op. cit. 440–54. A complete bibliography of Kelsen's writings in German, English, and French, listed both topically and chronologically, can be found in Robert Walter, *Hans Kelsen—Ein Leben im Dienste der Wissenschaft* (Vienna: Manz, 1985), 27–97, a volume in the series appearing under the auspices of the Hans Kelsen Institute, Vienna.

S. L. P.

Index of Names

Italic type marks references to the translators' material (preface, introduction, text notes, supplementary notes, biographical outline, and annotated bibliography), roman type, to Kelsen's text.

Index of Subjects

Entries are followed by page numbers rather than section numbers. Bold type flags a subject of unusual significance in Kelsen's text. Italicized page numbers mark references to the translators' material (preface, introduction, text notes, and supplementary notes).

Printed in the United Kingdom
by Lightning Source UK Ltd.
116912UKS00001B/20